WOMANKIND:

A CELEBRATION

And when the woman saw that the tree was good for food, and that it was pleasant to the eyes, and a tree to be desired to make one wise, she took the fruit thereof, and did eat, and gave also unto her husband with her; and he did eat. And the eyes of them both were opened.

Genesis

In just taking an apple off the tree and eating the whole thing, there are no mistakes to be made.

SHOJI HAMADA

Also by MICHAEL ADAM

Man is a Little World
A Matter of Death and Life
The Wild Strange Place
Wandering in Eden : Three Ways to
the East Within Us

WOMANKIND:

A CELEBRATION *by* MICHAEL ADAM

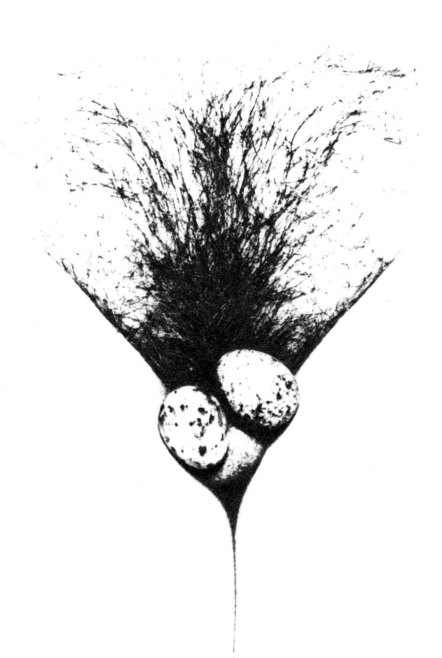

HARPER & ROW, PUBLISHERS
NEW YORK

Cambridge • Hagerstown • Philadelphia • San Francisco
London • Mexico City • São Paulo • Sydney

To Rosemary Manning, John & Antoinette Moat,
& for the family: Rani, Eya, Kim, Sue, Noah,
Shane, Nicholas; the many friends.

FIRST U.S. EDITION

Design by Kim Taylor

Library of Congress Catalog Card Number: 78-20623

ISBN: 0-06-090675-8 (Pbk) 79 80 81 82 83 10 9 8 7 6 5 4 3 2 1
ISBN: 0-06-010032-X 79 80 81 82 83 10 9 8 7 6 5 4 3 2 1

FRONT COVER. Robert Wyss : *Maya*
BACK COVER. Russell Lee : Italian peasant
PAGE 1. Eric Gill : *Adam and Eve*
TITLE PAGE. Sam Haskins, photograph (detail)
ABOVE. Ben Shahn, drawing
OPPOSITE. Thomas Bewick : *Nest*

CONTENTS

Introduction

A philosophy which shuts its eyes to the creative fire in man's nature — to the Eros or frenzy — cuts man's soul off from the fresh bodily earthy effects of life . . . and from the aesthetic and spiritual of man's nature.

JOSE CLEMENTE OROZCO

Perfection is a masculine desideratum, while woman inclines by nature to completeness . . . just as completeness is always imperfect, so perfection is always incomplete, and therefore represents a final state which is hopelessly sterile.

C.G. JUNG

To be perfect even as your Father in Heaven is perfect . . . Perfect? How was I to understand the word? Perfect and pure of heart? What means pure? Pure, pure . . . Pure apple juice! I began to sense a clue. Pure apple juice is made from the whole apple, bruises, blemishes, skin, core, the whole imperfect works. Pure apple juice is not pasturized, refined, filtered, nonentity! Bruises blemishes worms and all. To be perfect is to be whole, a paradox, even as our Father in Heaven, Behemoth and Leviathan, Christ and Satan . . .

MARY CAROLINE RICHARDS

He had been told that life was beautiful. No! Life is round.

JOE BOSQUET

THE NAKEDNESS OF WOMAN IS THE WORK OF GOD, said William Blake. The work of man, however, has always been to cover and clothe woman in every conceivable guise, to invest her with every virtue, every vice, so to imagine and make her in the shape of his innumerable needs of her. Woman is not permitted to be woman, simply; she is Mistress of Heaven, Queen Goddess of the World, and she is Kali, the Black One, bloody-tongued with a necklace of skulls about her neck. She is the Virgin, 'fair as the moon, elect as the sun', and she is Whore of All the World. She is bright Eve at the beginning, but her breasts are soon seen to gleam above the body of the Serpent. She is Sophia, the wisdom of God; she is Shakti, his energy. She is 'that Eternal Feminine who calls us on', and she is Maya, the illusion that holds us back. She is the world within, the very Soul of man, and she is the flesh into which the Word was made, the material world about us. She is the Sphinx. She is all manner of things to all manner of men: for Dante the leading light of Beatrice; for Saint Antony a dark strumpet who shadows him even into the bleakest desert. For most men woman is something of all these and more that is unnameable, unfathomable: death to those who fear to live; life to those who dare to die.

What woman *is*, we do not know; we cannot know. We can but come to see it, to allow it, to celebrate it.

To celebrate woman, however, is not to praise an ideal creature; it is to sing of the dark and of the light of her, to sing the whole woman. This is itself the way of the Feminine which allows all things as they are, mortal and imperfect, wholly so.

If the end is celebration, the beginning is information: facts and reflection upon facts to the end of reflection, the start of wonder in us.

OPPOSITE. Felix Hoffmann : *Womankind*

who, being wise about women, are careful to keep their distance.

There can be no claim to authority in unknowable matters. If credentials are needed, it may be said that as every man I was born of woman; as most men I have a wife; as many I have a daughter; as some, a grand-daughter. These and all other women I have in some way known are my mentors. There is also that Woman within me as in every man, the source and well-spring of all knowledge of a kind that is not only masculine and of the mind alone.

And there is then the world about me, the wide wild earth itself, the material world for which woman is said to stand. I wake each day to this world, enter and experience it under sun and shadow, in calm and in storm, in intimate relationship.

The equation of woman with the earth is old; there is an ancient link between landscape and her lying down, swelling hills with the breasts of her, thickets with her pubic hair, valley with vulva: 'Ile be a parke and thou shalt be my deere; feed where thou wilt, on mountain or in dale, graze on my lips, and if those hils be drie, stray lower, where the pleasant fountains lie.'[1]

ABOVE. Cyril Satorsky : *Sara*

BELOW. *The Pursuit of Wisdom* 17c

That a man should reflect upon Womankind is understandable; one is attracted by what seems wholly 'other', by what is unknown and even, as here, unknowable. A book about Woman that is without bewilderment and contradiction is not a book about Woman. Moreover, all that can be said about Woman may happily be disproved by each and every woman — infant, child, girl, wife, granny and crone, she beguiles and yet escapes all analysis, as the whistle of a strange bird in the night of a foreign wood.

I have wondered about Womankind and sometimes thoughts have come to me that can even seem a little wise. It is well that they are balanced by the folly of my own life and my being with women, else I might seek to emulate those sages

8

This association is not a matter of literature or of history only, is not accidental or only allegorical. Our attitudes to woman in large measure determine our attitudes to the world around us. No man at ease with woman will rape the earth, will use and abuse it, mechanically, chemically, economically.

And this is not all, for society reflects our wealth or want of womankindliness. Those abstract generalizations, ideas, ideals and principles which rule our lives and which can bring ruin and war to the world, are born in the minds of men who lack womankindly concern for particulars, for individuals, for things, for life itself. We are plagued by male authority in all its death-dealing procrustean forms, by planners who insistently order the world and the rest of us in their own ideal ways, but always for our *own* 'good', even though it shackles us, even if it kills us.

ABOVE. Jan Balet : *A-minor*

9

With so much of Woman within and about him, a man should not be a stranger to the subject; indeed, his understanding of himself is in large part his understanding of woman. To speak of woman as wholly 'other' is therefore mistaken. 'Perhaps sex is by itself a universal quality, undifferentiated except by its embodiment as wine takes the shape of its jug, but is still wine. So that men and women who have much of it have automatically more of what belongs to the other; and it is the very male men, the very female women, who most easily enter into each other's feelings.'[2]

H.G.Wells in 1920 said that the emancipation of women was one of the most important events of the twentieth century. More than half a century later, the statement seems mistaken only in its modesty. The need for the liberation of women is imperative now. The call comes clear from women today, and loud from those who march under the banner of *Women's Lib* — but there the word liberation is appropriately truncated. The story of man's inhumanity to woman is such that it should not surprise us if some women now shout about it, even though this cannot in the end serve the cause of women's liberation. If the need is for men to see women as they are, it is as much needed for women to see what they are *not*. Women have too often in a man's world assumed 'masculine' values and now, in protesting against oppression, ape their oppressors. Shouting is a 'masculine' way and in following it women allow themselves to be measured by 'masculine' standards and so dismissed by fearful men with derisive laughter. The liberation of women (as that of men) must be the wish of all humane persons, but liberation is not primarily activist or political; no man is an *ism*, no woman an *ist*.

ABOVE. Augustus John : *The Smiling Woman*

OPPOSITE. Anne Gauldin : *Women of Rudelle*, France

The need is for women who are women wholly — made whole, that is, by marriage with masculine aspects in them; even as the need is for men to be whole by way of inward marriage with their feminine selves. Women and men, not driven by an ideal of perfection but moved by the innate and natural need for wholeness, will rejoice in the differences between them, will delight in all diversity, in all the many parts that make the Whole. There is no way to world peace but that of individual women and men at ease in themselves and so with all about them.

Women who see equality with men as the achievement of happiness doom themselves to disappointment. Wrong conditions can be righted, but happiness does not lie in right conditions; it lies in being the right person even in wrong conditions. 'Feminism' therefore needs to be understood as the freedom of the Feminine in each of us and all about us. As such, it may well be *the* most important movement of our times. The fear and repression of the Feminine for over three thousand years has determined the very nature of our thinking, our attitudes and acts; it has shaped our religions, our morals, our marriages, the upbringing of our children, and has even led to wars and the suicidal exploitation of our planetary resources.

I speak of Womankind in the way that we have hitherto spoken of Mankind, meaning both women and men. There is an imbalance to redress so that my emphasis here is upon woman, though my real wish is to speak of Humankind, of women and men, that is, stripped of all false images and so able to delight in their real differences, well knowing their oneness all the while.

ABOVE. *Victory of Samothrace*, c.190BC

I am blessed by the friendship of a gentle Protestant priest, as by that of a faithful Catholic and of other good Christians who offer examples of a peace to be had by deeply kneeling to a God who is of old and is ever. Other friends point to gurus and to wise men of the East. But if I have learned anything from good and wise men, I have learned as much from women who, men often say, are fools. They may well be so since they can care for men and give themselves so carelessly to them.

This feminine ability 'to care and not to care' is not only the way of all right relationships, but also the way to that abundant life we individually lack. We begin by saying *Yes!* as women in love will do. The way of the Feminine is the way of faith, but faith in *nothing*, for faith in anything is only security, not faith at all. The way of womankindliness is the readiness to be given and taken in marriage with all that seems other than oneself, with life itself, all the dark and the light of it. Only by way of that willing engagement can there ever come about the inward marriage that is asked of us, of each woman and of every man.

A woman or a man in whom the marriage of masculine and feminine parts has come about, in whom all wayward disparate elements are embraced, is at once whole with the Whole of creation, with all

> *the astonishing beauty of things — earth, stone and water*
> *Beast, man and woman, moon and stars —*
> *The blood-shot beauty of human nature, its thoughts, frenzies and passions,*
> *And unhuman nature its towering reality . . .*[3]

ABOVE. Margaret Michaelis : Bodenweiser Ballet

OPPOSITE & BELOW. : Barbara Whitehead, woodcuts

NOTE: By *Feminine* and *Masculine* I mean throughout what are ordinarily understood as 'principles' (as the *Yin* and the *Yang* of the Chinese); by *feminine* and *masculine* I mean the way that these principles naturally work in the world; by *'feminine'* and *'masculine'* I mean the excess of either of these and the resultant imbalance that makes for a perversion of those first principles. That there should be some confusion is inevitable since there are no hard and fast distinctions. Real confusion is better than unreal clarity. The meaning of these ordinary words may seem vague and hard to grasp by the mind alone, but may be *felt* by anyone in their context, and without need of psychological or other forms of knowledge and reference.

REFERENCES

1. *The Song of Songs*
2. CARY, Joyce : *Selected Essays* Michael Joseph, London, 1976
3. JEFFERS, Robinson : 'The Beauty of Things' *Robinson Jeffers Selected Poems* Vintage Books, New York, 1965

ABOVE. *Priestess*. Card from Marseille Tarot pack

I *Woman, Kind and Unkind*

There is a dark principle in God himself.
JACOB BOEHME

Modern man, on a different plane, discovers what primordial man experienced through an overpowering intuition: namely that in the generating and nourishing, protective and transformative, feminine power of the unconscious, a wisdom is at work that is infinitely superior to the wisdom of man's waking consciousness . . . This feminine-maternal wisdom is not abstract disintegrated knowledge but a wisdom of loving participation . . . A spirit mother Sophia is not, like the Goddess Mother of the lower phase, interested primarily in the infant, the child and the immature man, who cling to her in these stages. She is rather the goddess of the Whole, who governs the transformation from the elementary to the spiritual level; who desires whole men knowing life in all its breadth, from the elementary phase to the phase of spiritual transformation.

ERICH NEUMANN

IN THE BEGINNING WAS THE WORD, it is written. The beginning itself was Woman. Before all beginnings and at the end of all endings, as in all the sweet and the bitter lingering of things, No-thing is, Emptiness IS. Its sign is that 'circle whose centre is everywhere and whose circumference is nowhere'.[1] It is formless, timeless, Whole and wholly inconceivable. It is in no way the absence of something or of the many things. It is Presence.

> Before creation a presence existed,
> Self-contained, complete
> Formless, voiceless, mateless,
> Changeless,
> Which yet pervaded itself
> With unending motherhood.
> Though there can be no name for it,
> I have called it 'the way of life'.
> Perhaps I should have called it 'the fullness of life',
> Since fullness implies widening into space,
> Implies still further widening,
> Implies widening until the circle is whole.
> In this sense
> The way of life is fulfilled,
> Heaven is fulfilled,
> Earth fulfilled,
> And a fit man also is fulfilled:
> There are four amplitudes of the universe
> And a fit man is one of them:
> Man rounding the way of earth,
> Earth rounding the way of heaven
> Heaven rounding the way of life
> Till the circle is full.[2]

The circle has always served as a sign of the totality of things, for Wholeness, since it is as a line drawn around all the many things, yet it is One. Holding all opposites without opposition, it is serene, contained, entire. The circle is round as the ring of the planets, as the spin of the earth about the sun, as the earth itself and the sun, as round as the face of a kitchen clock, and it is timeless.

OPPOSITE. Sam Haskins : *Eve*

17

In moments when we no longer look and so may be found, in the experiencing of that Whole which is always and only present, in such moments all images fall away, as the imagination does. 'Whereof one cannot speak, thereof one must be silent.'[3] One should, but while we are as we are, seemingly partial and haunted by the Wholeness that IS, we will feel the need to speak of it, as we must surely speak of all that stands in the way of it.

The part cannot conceive the Whole but out of the wish to do so (itself out of the need to *be* whole), the partial mind dismembers and distinguishes, gives a form to the formless, translates eternity into time.

So once upon a time, 'before time was', Oroborus was; the snake with its tail in its mouth making a full circle. Out of that One came the many, so that the circle could seem to some like the full belly of a woman who miraculously brings forth: 'When the heavens had not been formed, when the earth had not been named, Tiamat brought forth . . . Tiamat, Mother of the Gods, Creator of all.'[4]

Split within ourselves and separated from all about us, for all our immortal dreams as mortal as gnats, the circle has come to stand for a state of being from which we are said to have strayed, as it is one to which we aspire. Looking back, the circle can seem round as the wall about that Paradise Garden from which we are exiled; looking ahead it is as the halo about the heads of those who are whole as we must hope to be, and who are therefore held to be holy among us.

Popes in their palaces and street-walking whores, sages and fools, women and men, one and all, by way of women we come to light, make our entrances into the world. By way of woman we are then suckled and sustained, arched over by her care and smiling, so that for a while woman is the world for us: ground, surround, sun and sky. Although essentially whole and therefore androgyne, the Primal Deity would at the start of the world be given richly feminine form. Amplebreasted, with widespread hips and great gravid belly, the Mother Goddess had sway over all the infancy of humankind and conciousness.

LEFT ABOVE. *Urobourus*, symbol of the cyclic nature of the Universe, 'from the One to the One'
LEFT. *Venus of Willendorf*, Austria, paleolithic
OPPOSITE. John Emmanuel : *Pregnant model*

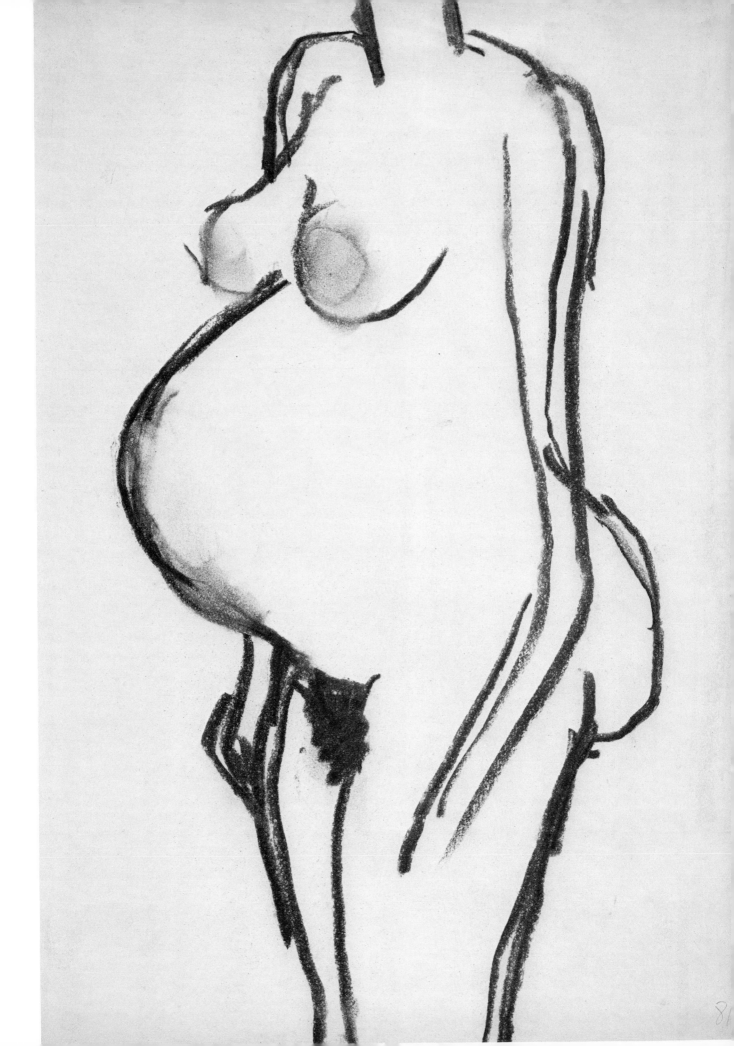

It was so when men roamed the earth in the track of wild creatures whose abundance was a gift of the Great Goddess and whose sacrifice meant life. How much more must have been man's regard for the Goddess when humankind began to settle, to put seeds deep into the dark earth and wait with faith upon their rot and resurrection.

The Goddess was then identified with the earth itself. The souls of children were thought by some to abide in the belly of the earth until they issued out of swamps and streams, caves and grottoes into bodies of women who had wandered there. *Vagina* for the Egyptians meant also the gallery of a mine leading into the earth. Once born of woman, the child was placed upon the earth, to be lifted up then by the man in gratitude to the Goddess whose creation the human mother only completed.

Only that, but how much that was! It was no small matter that by way of a holy place and her own body, the woman was related to that mysterious Whole out of which all came, by which all existed, to which all returned in the end. In the compelling drag of man's desire for woman, the want that overwhelmed him and brought him down to her, in the blood that flowed from every woman as regularly as the moon, in its sudden cease and her swelling and in time bringing to unaccountable birth, in all dark and instinctual ways, woman was a party of Mystery as no man. A man might run and draw a bow, carry back on his wide shoulders the slain body of a beast; he might do many necessary things, but nothing numinous; he had skills but no secrets.

LEFT. *Goddess*, Susa, 7BC

20

RIGHT. Mary Beth Edelson : Great Goddess Series, 1975. 'Reaching across the centuries we take the hand of our ancient Sisters.'

BELOW. Charles Roff : *Cave 1*

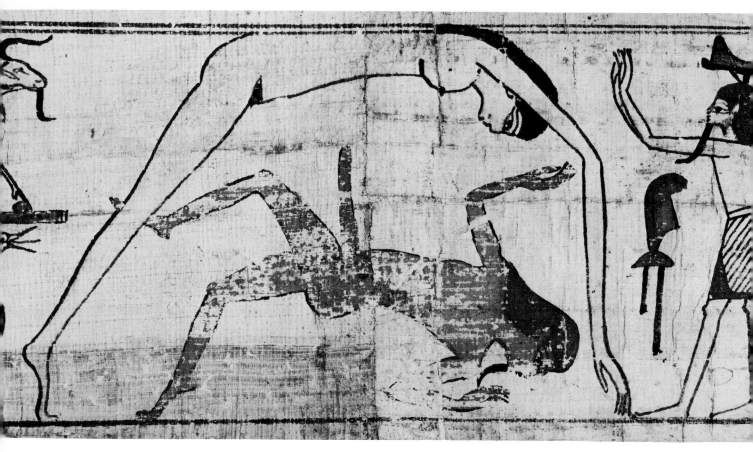

ABOVE. *Nut, Goddess of Sky, separated from Geb, the Earth-God.* Egypt, 11th dynasty

RIGHT BELOW. *Virgin Birth* : Nut (the Sky) gives birth to the Sun; its rays fall on Hathor in the Horizon (Love and Life)

OPPOSITE ABOVE. *The Flower of the Wise*, 1550. In the Hermetic egg lies the dragon Urobourus; out of this egg grows the red flower of gold, the white of silver, and, between them, the blue flower of the wise.

The sun's part in the penetration of the earth, in procreation, would not at the start be known. The heavens were not formed. But with man's realization of his part in the making of other men and women, the image of the origin of things could be revised. Now it could seem round as a woman and a man in a single shape, hermaphrodite; or as a line drawn about two lovers: 'In the beginning this world was Self, whole and alone. Looking around, It saw nothing else. It said: *I am*, and was, indeed, large as a woman and a man in close embrace.' But in order that creation might come about, there must be two, the opposites must be. 'The Self caused Itself to fall into two parts. Therefrom arose a wife and a husband.'[5] The World Parents came into being, Mother Earth and Father Sky.

The heavens were now formed, but the heavens were still far; earth was at hand and

22

under foot. The Goddess still played the major part: 'In the heavens I take my place and send rain; in the earth I take my place and cause the green to spring forth.' The Goddess also caused the want of all creatures for one another: 'I turn the male to the female, I turn the female to the male. I am she who adorneth the male for the female, I am she who adorneth the female for the male.'

Out of the fulfilment of that want came not only the multitude of things but the exuberance and excess of them — the unnecessary sputter of larks and singing of seals, the unending hurl and hush of the sea, the burn of the tiger and the grace of some young girl singing for no good reason, the sway and leap of women and men in the dance, and death all the while uncalled for, everywhere — all the tender and lively terror of things, the aweful beauty.

'The spirit comes from the body of the world.'[6] Whatever man has thought or brought of worth to the world has root in this world, rises out of matter (more immaterial, we know now, than we could ever have imagined); all comes from the earth, out of the dark of the body, of womanly being, from the Feminine, that is, and by way of that impelling love which is the way of the Feminine and which links the body's evolution and the emergence of its consciousness with the history of culture. Out of the crude needs of shelter, of bloody meat and rape, woman-kindliness has shaped the home, the ceremonies of the table and the celebrations of the bed. Then as now:

> My husband comes across
> The fields to dine.
> The hot coals he brings me
> I cover with myrtle.[7]

Now as ever men rage and wander, come and go as they sometimes must, but woman out of her natural link with the way of the earth and with her body in the service of small children will incline to stay. Staying is the start of all civility.

RIGHT. The cross of Christ growing as a blue lily out of the Virgin. 'The lily corresponds to the Quintessence, and the Mother of God to *materia prima*.' TITUS BURCKHARDT

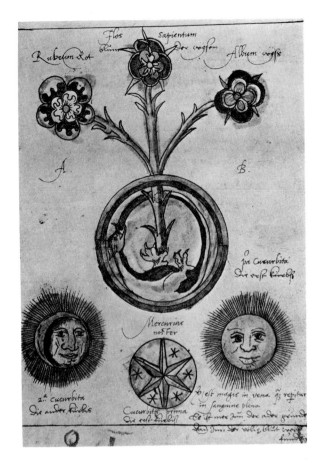

BELOW LEFT. *The Sun God's birth from a flower*, Egypt. 'Birth from the female blossom is an archetypal form of divine birth.' ERICH NEUMANN

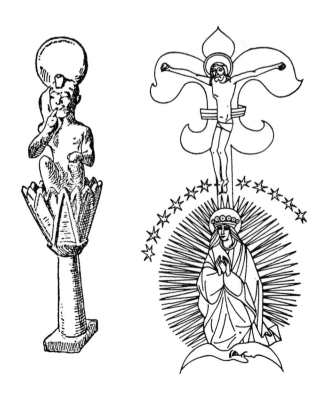

hundred years brought to light shows ancestors by no means only brutal. Even those who lived in caves were not content to do so: they painted the walls, and as much as thirty thousand centuries after, the bison of Altamira still majestically roams, the horses, deer and bulls of Lascaux go swiftly as ever, and elsewhere men still hunt and women on those walls still dance. The handprints of women have been found among these images of unaccountable genius and in the low-ceilinged sleeping quarters, so that the images may well have been the work of women, painted simply for the joy of it perhaps, without that masculine purpose and solemn meaning so often ascribed to them, and no less numinous for that.

The history of civilization as told by man has, however, until recently begun with man's dominance on earth as in heaven where a Father God sat as an emperor enthroned, high and apart. Before that Authority and Order, the story tells, there was Chaos; and until the establishment of a similar authority on earth in all religious and secular matters, there was a like chaos, with man at the mercy of his brutal and ungoverned impulses, and therefore prey to woman.

And yet there have been haunting myths of vanished civilizations, crystal centres of once upon a time, legends of lost islands under the sea, of a Golden Age lived without fear of the gods, in ease and natural order, without need of laws and so without deceit and treachery; no deep moats about the towns, no swords, no trumpets since there was no call to conquer. Uncompelled, the earth gave sustenance and other needs were satisfied since all was shared, and the wildness of love was allowed to all until death was given as a gentle sleep at life's end — all this under the aegis of that Goddess whose image has been found everywhere from the Siberian wastes to the mountains of Spain and the island of Malta.

These legends, embellished by longing and by despair in our own lives and times, have been dismissed as the dreams of unruly poets. The evidence cannot. All that the spade has in the past

LEFT. Edward Calvert : *A Primitive City*, 1872
BELOW. *Fertility Goddess*, Mycenaean, 7c BC

24

BELOW. Cave paintings, Lascaux

ABOVE. Stone drawing, Algeria, paleolithic. 'Male hunter magically connected, from genital to genital, with a female figure with upraised arms – a clear expression of the magical function of the Feminine.'
ERICH NEUMANN

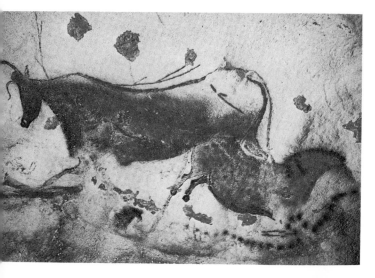

And when women and men gathered in greater numbers to live together, it is clear from all the evidence that they fished and hunted; ate and drank from pots and pans they were not content to eat and drink from; they painted them too; they created, painted, carved, danced and in their own way loved one another. There is nothing to suggest that they warred. The influence of women may be assumed. Her ability to create life and her innate need to foster it, not by quantitative increase only but qualitatively by enrichment, will have worked to soften and still man's angry restless spirit.

ABOVE. *Dance Group*, rock painting, Spain

In all areas of the archaic world under the watch of the Mother Goddess and the ward of women, it was apparently so: peace in Egypt of the Old Kingdom, in early Sumer and ancient Crete. Things of useful beauty, little and large, fashioned of clay and stone, of silver and gold have been found in buildings unsurpassed by subsequent ages until the Greeks. Due worship was given there always to images of fertility and to the generative forces, to love in the service of life, and the people's daily lives will have reflected their religion. Love must be since life will be. The Cretan Goddess bared herself saying: *I have breasts. I am.* The women of the island were without shame and dressed provocatively. Such societies, it is clear, were governed by some livelier principle than morality and rigid patriarchal rule.

Whether or not such societies were truly matriarchal has been a matter of dispute among scholars. Understanding that extremes imply their opposites, the historian J.J.Bachofen concluded that 'the strictness of the patriarchal system points to an earlier system that had to be combatted and suppressed.' He was led to the study of myths of the Great Mother and her rule in archaic Greece, seeing in these 'a manifestation of primordial thinking, an immediate historical revelation, and consequently a highly reliable source'. His findings joined 'to form a single picture' and led to the conclusion that matriarchy is not confined to any particular people, but marks a cultural stage, preceding that of the patriarchal system.[8]

There have been objections. It might be allowed that such societies were matriarchal if it did not also seem clear that they were, by all civilized standards, utopian. Together with the fact that there is not one Father-God figure among all the many images from earliest times, there is evidence of the kind unearthed in Catal Huyuk, a site that covers more than thirty acres of modern Turkey. Dating back as much as ten thousand years, it is the most ancient town we know, and: 'There had been no war for a thousand years. There was an ordered pattern of society. There were no human or animal sacrifices. Vegetarianism prevailed, for domestic animals were kept for milk and wool — not for meat. There is no evidence of violent deaths . . .

Above all the supreme deity in all the temples was a goddess.'[9]

'Mother of all the gods' sang Lucretius of her, 'Sole mistress of all things, without whom nothing can be glad or lovely.' Or be at all. To those ancient womankindly ages, we owe food, clothing and shelter as we have come to rejoice in them; we owe fire and its use, pottery, weaving, building, the invention of the wheel; to woman we owe agriculture, and the debt is not only for grains and fruits but also for what was allowed by the provision of these in excess of daily needs: the time, that is, to do nothing, to dream of greater deeds, of ships and cities and the making of things. We owe to these ages the necessary art of numbers and the essential flute; we owe music, literature, all the arts and, for good and ill, much of our religions; to these ages we owe our humanity.

'The oldest of our words refer to the work of women, and more than that: "Who will continue to ask why . . . all the qualities that embellish man's life are known by feminine names? Why justice, peace, intelligence, wisdom, rectitude, devotion, liberty, mercy, intellect, nobility, concern, gentleness, clemency, generosity, kindliness, dignity, spirit, soul, freedom — all, all are feminine" . . . This choice is no free invention or accident, but is an expression of historical truth . . . The accord between historical facts and the linguistic phenomenon is evident . . . Women were the originators and repositories of all culture . . . and the source of the first civilization.'[10]

OPPOSITE ABOVE. *Head of a Princess*, from Tel el Amarna, 1370–60BC
OPPOSITE BELOW. *Torso*, probably from Tel el Armana, 1370–60BC
RIGHT. *Aphrodite*, Graeco-Roman

If once upon a time it was all so good and true, it was too good to be true forever. What is true to its time becomes a lie beyond that time. For its while in the womb, the embryo knows Nothingness, is rounded and whole. Once born, the infant breaks apart. The pain of separation is, however, alleviated by the mother's full breast and loving care; although the One is no longer, the two can seem as one.

The breach widens, as it must. The child must grow and go alone, and goes eagerly for the most part as to a new adventure. And yet all the while out of the accompanying wish to be as of old and one with the mother, he goes with fear and trembling as to his death, sensing that to live and grow is to die to all that is old and sure and known.

The adolescent not only turns from the mother, but may turn against her. She is the old link that he must sever if he is to live newly; the dark from which he must save himself if he is to come to light at all. The Good Mother may, therefore, come to assume for him the mask of Evil. He takes up arms as a hero.

Whatever else they may be, myths are states of mind. The emerging of man's consciousness is told in all the tales of bright heroes contending with dark demonic forces. The awareness of these forces is the end of childhood and the beginning of adult consciousness; the readiness to face them is the birth of the hero.

The mother who was a guardian at the start comes in time to show other aspects. She may try to hold the child to her forever, as one part of the child may even wish, but as the livelier part will know cannot be. But even if the mother wishes only the good of her child and so its growth and going from her, she will come nevertheless to reveal a shadow side. She is absent sometimes when most needed; she may prevent or punish; in weaning she withholds and so denies; she may even in some dark way be desired and so is in that way denied. The child at the start knows only love for the mother; if it is to be more than a child, it must know more; it may know hate.

LEFT ABOVE. Embryo in womb. From a manuscript on the teachings of Soranus, a Greek physician
ABOVE. *The walled Garden of Paradise*; the form is of a womb that they must leave if they are to live

The embrace of the Feminine includes all things. So the mother who seems at the start the source of all light, in time brings knowledge of the shadow that haunts all things. The Feminine is the creative force of life and as such cannot be always and invariably kind; she is always necessary if there is to be life at all and growth. Our wish to see the Feminine in the best light only, as with the image of the Virgin Mary, is the measure of our refusal to grow. It is to deny the full transforming power of the Feminine, the threat she poses to all who would remain in her elementary embrace, would stay as sucklings, or allow her to devour them. Images from all times all over the world remind us of the other side of the Good Mother: Medusa with her serpent hair, Rangda with staring eyes, Kali, black and bloody-tongued.

She may be a vampire in our dreams or haunt the hero with sweetest singing, be a siren holding him back from his journey, keeping him from consciousness, be as the Lady of the House of Sleep.

The hero is one who for all his fear, for all longing and looking back, for all loneliness, yet goes forward alone, Prince of the Lonesome Isle. If he is ever to be individual, undivided, he must first know division in him. Consciousness at the start is consciousness of separation; a cord must be cut so that there will seem to be two things: oneself and all that one is not, the Other which must be confronted. 'The other is hell,' said Sartre. It was well said, if only of this stage.

BELOW. William Blake : *Hecate*, Goddess of the dark and the underworld, mistress of ghosts and spectres

Gone from the safe but restricting circle of the Mother, the hero turns to the Father. Chaos is the country of the Feminine, the dark from which he must come. The way out and into the world is by way of the Father and by the masculine will to dare and do. 'The light, the light, the seeking, the searching in chaos, in chaos.'[11] The masculine mind is the principle and agent of discrimination, of resolution and decision; the mind is as a sword in the hero's hand.

Later the hero will come to realize that the dark is not apart from himself, that the dread Minotaur is at the centre of the maze of his own mind, and if he enters with a sword in his right hand, he will emerge with the help of the Feminine, the thread of Ariadne in his left hand.

But going forward now, he goes with the Father in mind, to slay what now seems to be evil, to save what now seems to be good. 'The patriarchal point of view is distinguished from the earlier archaic view by its setting apart of all pairs-of-opposites — male and female, life and death, true and false, good and evil — as though they were absolutes in themselves and not merely aspects of the larger unity of life.'[12]

But illusory views are not ended by the statement that they are illusions. Illusions, while we have them, are what we *are*. They can only be lived out. History is the living out of our illusions. Whatever else it may be, history is first an inner happening.

LEFT ABOVE. Labyrinth scratched on a painted pillar in the house of Lucretius, Pompeii, before AD79
LEFT. Theseus battles with the Minotaur at the centre of the Labyrinth, 12c

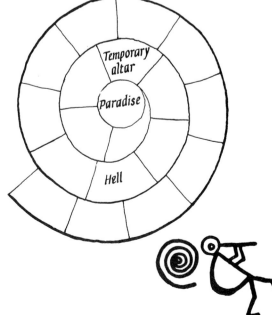

OPPOSITE LEFT BOTTOM. Labyrinthine 'Mother Earth'
symbol of the Hopi Indians
OPPOSITE RIGHT. Warriors emerging from the
Labyrinth. Etruscan jar, 7c BC
ABOVE. Sandro Botticelli : Illustration to Dante's
Inferno, 16c. 'To gain full experience of the Way he
comes; wherefore behoves him to be led . . . Gyre
after gyre through Hell.'
RIGHT. Drawing of French form of children's game of
Hopscotch – in Germany called *Tempel-* or
Himmelhüpfen (Temple- or Heaven-hopping)
RIGHT BELOW. Hump-backed flute player, Hopi Indian

So it was that the necessary emergence from unconsciousness manifested itself in time as the Patriarchal Revolution that in the end overwhelmed the old world of the Great Mother. It was not suddenly done. Nor was it a matter of evil at once replacing good. As the child emerges slowly from the magic circle of the mother, so humankind will have moved slowly away from the Goddess and from matriarchal rule. It was not ended simply by imposition and cruel invasion from outside forces, but as much from inward failure. When matriarchy ceased to be organic, it became institutional and so brought about its own decay. If, as J.J. Bachofen said, an earlier system had to be combatted, it suggests that there was reason to combat it. The excesses of the patriarchal system point to equal excesses of the matriarchal system.

All systems are excessive. Nature shows no system, but a lively balancing of contrary forces. At the beginning was woman and her influence will have been strong in all early societies, whether of hunting tribes or small settlements, making for peace and organic order. Such societies still exist today to show that war is not the outcome of a savage instinct that civilization has tempered — a view which the Church has understandably upheld and to which Freud has contributed — but that civilization is itself a cause of war.

The increase in size of early settlements with the consequent increase in the need for control will have brought laws and so lawbreakers, so more and stronger laws imposed from above. Organic order will have been replaced by that authoritarian order without which war is impossible.

The Great Mother had been accessible to all by common feelings of awe and gratitude. In time, however, there appeared those who appointed themselves her mediators and representatives, and matriarchal rule in the increasing measures of its ruling, grew more and more rigid and excessive'; it grew, paradoxically, more 'masculine'.

The necessary sacrifice of a beast to feed a family for its life's sake became in time a religious act, not only in the avowed service of the Mother Goddess, but also for the sake of the State and the welfare of society — two very different ends whose confusion we suffer to this day.

Animal sacrifices then gave way to human sacrifice. Life came from the Goddess and depended upon her; man was needed but was expendable. The Priestess was representative of the Goddess, but her consort after a year of service was sacrificed at the height of his powers lest the corn wither with him. Understandably, such sacrifices were not welcomed by all, and with the increasing power of the King the substitution of others will have suggested itself — bright virgins and beautiful youths of the tribe or, better still, those of another tribe. The need for victims from abroad will have brought the need for war, and the very act of sacrifice will have made for that indifference to human values which allows wars, now as then.

Then as now, that indifference will have been reasoned away and even given religious justification, being claimed as a necessary means to a noble, ideal end. The reasoning will have been done by male priests who even then in the service of the Goddess were gaining power by imitation and identification with her priestesses by castrating themselves or, less drastically, by becoming celibate and adopting women's clothing, as is done to this day.

OPPOSITE. David Jones : *Aphrodite in Aulis*

33

The emergence from the early age of womanly influence will have taken place over centuries. Although the end of some cities will have been swift, bloody and brutal (a scribe of the Third Dynasty at Ur wrote of 'a host whose onslaught was like a hurricane, a people who had never known a city'), the matriarchal Golden Age was not everywhere at once replaced by a patriarchal Iron Age of aggression. There will most surely have been, metaphorically speaking, a Silver Age of early civilizations when the seeds of war were being sown, and a Bronze Age when the civilized ills of acquisitiveness, envy, social division and aggression rankly flowered under the Sun and Sky Gods who were gradually replacing the Moon and Earth Goddesses of earlier matri-archies.

The moon in her many moods told men of both eternity and transience. Born out of the dark, the bright new moon still held the dark in her arms, and coming in time to full light and form, then died and returned to the dark, only to be resurrected and return, over and over. Dark and light, as earth and sky, as death and life, were of a mysterious Whole that was not to be comprehended by man because he was a part of it.

The sun, by strong contrast, could seem to allow nothing of the dark; transcendent and assertive, it conquered darkness, dispelled all mystery by its presence. The priests of the Sun and the Sky Gods turned from the old easy ways of the earth, of plant and animal life and the mysterious interdependence of all things, to a new kind of order suggested by the sky where the movements of stars and planets seemed exact and calculable, an order that could be determined and so could be enforced. We have inherited this 'masculine' attitude; it has directed all our achievements in science, technology and much else that has been of inestimable benefit. Unless counter-balanced now, it could determine our end.

Felix Hoffmann : Illustrations for a Picture Bible

It is certain that it determined the end of those many civilizations that had long flourished under Feminine care. The first invasions will have been absorbed and for long centuries the old worship continued with new male gods subservient: the Sun God joining with the Earth Goddess in the same service of Life and of society. In time, however, the 'masculine' craving for power and absolute mastery will have brought conflict and turned the Sun God into a God of War. With the crude will to conquer ennobled then as now by high-sounding ideals and religious sanction, all forms of butchery, rape and devastation became permissible means to the noble ends of a crusade that would bring the Light of God to the dark realm of the Goddess. So it was told in one of the Dead Sea Scrolls, *The Scroll of the Sons of Light Against the Sons of Darkness*: 'The first engagement of the Sons of Light shall be to attack the Sons of Darkness . . . The Sons of Light are the lot of God.'

From the north came a wild people who then spread east and west. As Aryans they poured into the Indus valley; as Celts they went to ancient Crete where the Goddess had for so long stood with bare breasts, defenceless and easy to rape.

But it was the Semites who finally put an end to the rule of the Goddess in the west, and to the old regard for women that accompanied her worship. The Semites brought the new myth of a single male Creator who did not cause the world in the way of nature and of the female, by birth, growth and nourishing, but by sudden supernatural command: 'God said let there be light, and there was light. And God saw that the light was good: and God divided the light from the darkness.' The dark was therefore an evil to be eliminated, an attitude that still infects us.

With that ample-breasted, wide-hipped, open-armed and imminent Goddess replaced by a stern and jealous Jehovah in high heaven, it was easy to justify the bloody ways of that God's emissaries, the male kings and rulers. They were simply obeying orders from on high: 'You must completely destroy all the places where the nations you dispossess have served their gods, on high mountains, on hills, under any spreading tree . . .'[13] Obediently, 'Joshua massacred the population of the whole region . . . He left no survivor, destroyed everything that drew breath as the Lord God of Israel commanded.'[14] There were some protests: 'Then all the men

which knew that their wives had burned incense to other gods and all the women that had stood by,' answered Jeremiah, 'As for the word that thou has spoken unto us in the name of the Lord, we will not hearken to thee. But we will certainly do whatsoever thing goeth forth out of our own mouth, to burn incense unto the Queen of Heaven, and to pour out drink offerings unto her, as we have done . . . for *then* had we plenty of victuals and were well and saw no evil. But since we left off to burn incense to the Queen of Heaven, and to pour out drink offerings unto her, we have wanted all things, and have been consumed by the sword and by the famine.'[15]

But with the Lord God on the side of the righteous and with iron weapons in hand, the issue was not in doubt. The bloody tale is told in and between the lines of the Old Testament. Thus saith the Lord: 'I have likened the daughter of Zion to a comely and delicate woman . . . Prepare ye war against her . . . Behold a people cometh from the north country. And a great nation shall be raised from the sides of the earth. They shall lay hold on bow and spear; they are cruel and have no mercy; their voice roareth as the sea and they ride on horses, set in array as men for war against thee, O daughter of Zion.'

So it came about: 'Lo, the fruitful place was a wilderness. And all the cities thereof were broken down in the presence of the Lord, and by his fierce anger'[17] . . . 'How doth the city sit solitary, that was full of people! How is she become as a widow! she that was great among nations . . . She weepeth sore in the night, and there are tears on her cheeks . . . For the Lord hath afflicted her . . . hath trodden the virgin, the daughter of Judah, as in a wine press . . . The Lord hath done that which he had devised . . . he hath thrown down and hath not pitied.'[18]

For all on the winning side, for those in obedient service to him, the Lord had assurances: 'I shall satiate the souls of the priests with fatness, and my peoples shall be satisfied with my goodness.' A single voice, however, a lone woman's, could not be stilled: 'A voice was heard in Ramah, lamentation and bitter weeping; Rachel weeping for her children refused to be comforted for her children, because they were not.'[19]

Christians of the first centuries after Jesus furthered the suppression of all the old ways of worship; some even giving authority to their cruel acts by putting into the mouth of Christ as in *The Gospel According to the Egyptians* the declaration: 'I have come to destroy the works of the female.'

The third western religion, born of the same impulse as Judaism and Christianity, was brought by Mohammed to seventh-century Arabia with the replacement of the ancient worship of the Goddess Al Lat by that of the one God Allah, and it was affirmed: 'Allah will not tolerate idolatory . . . the pagans pray to females.'

The ending of the worship of the Mother Goddess and her replacement by a Father God was not a simple event of history, not only the replacement of one rule by another, an exchange of idols. The nature of the Feminine and that of the Masculine, being complementary, are profoundly different, so that it will affect all if one is upheld and the other rejected. Man's conception of deity has determined the course of whole civilizations and given shape to the lives of all who have part in them. It still does, affecting even those who no longer subscribe to a god of any kind. The consequences of the patriarchal conquest of the western world do not need to be imagined; they are all about us.

The ancient world of the Great Mother had embraced all forms of natural life and all within a living Whole from which the sacred could not be separated. Deity was everywhere, mysterious yet plainly manifest, immanent in one and all and so immediately accessible.

The modern world of the Father, however, was born in a desert and in the minds of the wandering tribes of the Hebrews for whom nature had little to offer. Survival depended not upon the bounty of the earth but upon the solidarity of the tribe. This could be assured only by the authority of its elders and by obedience to leaders to whom all looked up. For ultimate authority they looked higher still to a Supreme Being far above the sandy wastes that surrounded them: God and man, the sacred and the natural were set apart. And like the bearded elders who conceived the image of that God, he was incontrovertibly male.

Lack of a bountiful homeland together with the need for survival's sake to invade the lands of others, and so sometimes to suffer defeat and captivity, all made for a desperate belief in a tribal God. Religion was racial. The realm of the sacred was no longer this world suffused through and through with a timeless ever-present Reality, but was the story of a particular God's intervention on behalf of a particular people in acts against their enemies. In such minds there grew sharp distinctions between good and evil, and all other opposites were set in opposition. Moreover, even as God was set apart in space, so fulfilment was put away in time. The world was to be suffered until a time when all would be well, and for that ideal distant future all men must live and strive. Inheriting this attitude, St Paul was later to say: 'I consider that the sufferings of the present time are not worth comparing with the glory that is to be revealed to us.'

Under the rule of a distant male God and separated from nature, man was also separated from his own nature and from the Feminine in him which, being suppressed, became malevolent. Women were essential for the continuance of the tribe, but they were clearly in league with nature and so less prone to the moral purposes of God and man, to law and to imposed order. They were, moreover, beguiling attendants of that desire which in Hesiod's words 'softens the sinews and overpowers the prudent purposes of the mind'. In contrast to the codes and practices of neighbouring peoples, the women of the Hebrews were constrained by cruel laws and made the property of men. It was decreed by Levite law that all women must be virgins before marriage and faithful forever after to a husband who could have as many wives as he wanted and whatever else he wished. Loss of virginity could bring stoning to death, as adultery did, even to the victim of rape. For the man, however, the rape of a virgin constituted a declaration of ownership. Understandably, even now the orthodox Hebrew man repeats the daily prayer: 'Blessed art thou, O Lord, our God, King of the Universe, who has not made me a woman.'

The way of men in such matters was 'divinely decreed'. The laws of the tribe were from on high, as the scriptures that revealed the word of God made clear. But such scriptures, we now know, took shape over many centuries and were made up of the myths and legends of the tribe, together with some adapted from other eastern peoples. To these were added events of history as well as the hopes of the Hebrews for themselves. The holy scriptures were therefore not even a simple compilation, but the work of priests who devoutly expunged all of which they did not approve and which did not fit their story of a chosen people under the special care of the one Supreme Being.

Felix Hoffmann : Illustrations for a Picture Bible

37

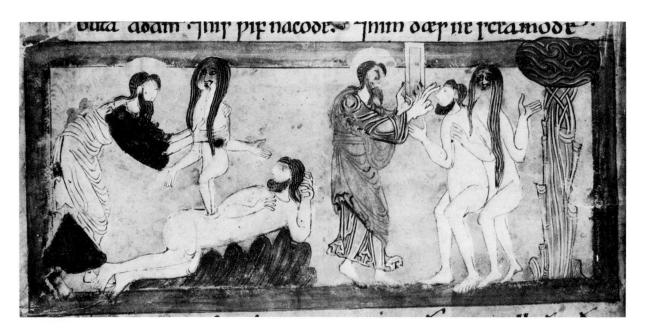

ABOVE. *The Creation of Eve*, 15c

BELOW. *The Garden of Immortality*. A mortal woman at left receives fruit of the Tree from dual apparition of the underworld deity, Gula-Bau. From a Babylonian cylinder seal, C1750–1550BC

This solitary Being, by his own confession 'a jealous God', was the special creation of the Hebrews. He was male and this sanctioned male supremacy on earth. Lest this might be mistaken as the invention of man, it needed to be established from the start of the world. A new and unique myth of creation was therefore invented: one in which the Feminine played no good part, neither as Goddess nor as woman.

To tell of this it was necessary to oppose all the natural order of things. Since the natural order was the realm of the Goddess, this presented no difficulty. Man was said to have been made as is no other form of life on earth, by supernatural act. As an afterthought only, and only from a spare rib of this man, woman was made. And this was presented not as a myth in the manner of other peoples' dreams of their beginning, but as a certain fact of history. The same insistence on history — in the place of myths that might be meaningfully interpreted and lived in the present moment — has already proved the death of Christianity for many, since literal belief in unnatural acts such as virgin birth and bodily assumption into heaven is still held by some to be the basis of any claim to be Christian.

Until about a century ago, it was widely held that the book of Genesis was the true story of the

creation of the world. A bishop was even able to determine that it happened 'in the night preceding the 23rd October, being our Sunday, in the year 4004BC'. At the root of the story was the wish to discredit all the older myths of the Earth Goddess held by other races.

The altars of the Goddess had been set up in groves with a sacred Tree, and the old myths associated this Tree with the Goddess herself. To eat of the fruit of the Tree was to partake of the body of the Goddess, and she was sometimes shown within the Tree offering its sacred fruit to the dead so that they might have immortality and have understanding of what 'only the gods knew'. The myth of the Hebrews also told of trees in the centre of the Garden, but to eat of their fruit was forbidden lest man should come upon knowledge and immortal life and so be as God.

The Serpent who had wound about the arms of the Goddess, representing wisdom and showing the way of renewal in the shedding of its old skin, was in the new myth cursed by God. The serpent (in early Christian art given the head and breasts of a woman) proved God to be a liar in his telling Adam and Eve that they would die of the sin of disobedience: 'Your eyes will be opened,' the Serpent said, 'and you will be like God, knowing good and evil.' Adam and Eve lived and with wide eyes now knew their nakedness. The Goddess had only encouraged nakedness and sexual knowledge, but this was now associated with disobedience to God and so became a matter of sin and of shame.

ABOVE. Arabella Ross : *Naked and Unashamed*, flour-dough plaque, 1977
BELOW. *Eve*, Autun, 12c

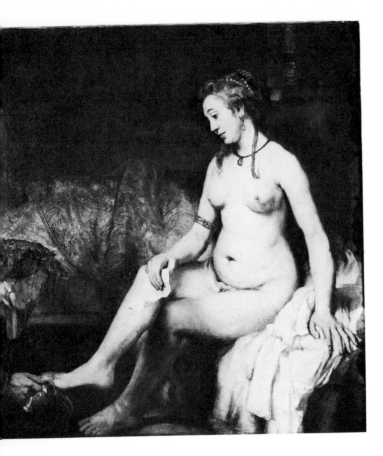

Adam's ready acceptance of the apple does not suggest a superior moral being, but the blame for his misbehaviour was squarely laid upon Eve. 'Do you not know,' the Christian lawyer Tertullian in the second century told an audience of women, 'that each of you is also an Eve . . . the devil's gateway . . . how easily you destroyed man, the image of God! Because of the death which you brought upon us, even the son of God had to die.'

Together with woman, the good earth itself, realm of the Goddess, was denigrated, turned to dust. 'Dust thou art,' Adam was told, 'and unto dust shalt thou return.'

The abuse of the Goddess and of all associated with her was thorough. There are few signs of womankindliness in the Old Testament; a few references to golden women like Ruth, gleaning in the field after the reapers, Bathsheba and the naked Susannah, 'a delicate woman and beauteous to behold', upon whom the lecherous elders gazed. But such women are matched by harridans: Jezebel, Delilah with a strong man's hair in her hands, and Salome with a good man's head.

ABOVE. Rembrandt : *Bathsheba at her toilet*

Cyril Satorsky : Illustrations to *The Song of Songs*

You have two round breasts like fawns to stroke, the twins of a shy gazelle . . . My beloved is an apple-tree heavy with fruit . . . His eyes, too, are doves dipping in clear water . . . His rod is arrogant ivory . . . Our bed is the living green.' Love is landscape. The exact description of any individual body must include a description of its immediate surrounds, and that environment is described by *its* surrounds so that there is no stopping short of the universe. Any one body is the whole body of the Universe, and that, we are told, is endless. Lovers are not blind when, in singing of one another, they include all creation.

Like a Susannah among elders who have not been content to pry, *The Song of Songs* has been interpreted by many, has been jostled and pummelled, stretched upon the rack of dogma, shame and superstition; has been raped by scholars and priests, theologians, apologists, earnest exegetists who all insist that it means other than it so simply says. Those who love will smile at it all as if with the words, if not the whole meaning, of Bernard of Clevaux: 'If any of those who read it desires to attain to a knowledge of it, let him love.'

But then, surprisingly, in the midst of it all there are signs of spring, 'the flowers appear on the earth'. In the Bible's midst is a small girl, black and comely, and in praise of her all the loveliness of the earth is invoked. As a lily among brambles, *The Song of Songs* appears among the opaque pages of the Old Testament, improbably as a rose in the cellar of a ruin; exempt from the centuries of guile and war, the fulminations of the prophets, the fret of kings, the fevers of a nation — a love song simply, sung among the groves and gardens, hills and plains of Palestine, but essentially out of time and place, the way of a maid and a man anywhere. Among the many lamentations for the loss of a people's favour with a jealous God, we find a girl crying only: 'Have you seen him I love with all my heart?' And amidst the sycophantic eulogies on that vengeful God, we find the shameless celebration of the body of a woman and that of a man: 'A spring of delight you are that makes life fertile, a well of living water . . . Your belly is a heap of wheat . . .

For further signs of the Feminine we must turn to the pages of the New Testament, to the person of Jesus and the things he is said to have said, which seem so alien to the old patriarchal attitudes in their telling of a new God who 'made the sun to rise on the evil and the good, and sendeth rain on the just and the unjust . . . Which of you by taking thought can add one cubit to his stature? Consider the lilies of the field. They toil not, neither do they spin. And yet I say unto you that even Solomon in all his glory was not arrayed as one of these. Behold the fowls of the air, for they sow not neither do they reap. Take no thought for the morrow . . . Love thy enemies . . .'

The words of Jesus and the image of him have been used by good and evil men to work for good and evil. Who Jesus was and what he said we cannot know. The earliest writings of Christianity are not the gospels written forty years after his death (the only recorded fact of his life), but the epistles of Paul. If Christianity owed its first impulse to the being of Jesus, it took its eventual shape from the mind of Paul, a very different man, who only twenty years after the Crucifixion was already railing at opponents who 'preach another Jesus', meaning, it seems, those who knew Jesus at first hand and saw in him the Messiah of Israel.

Paul, who had been violently anti-Christian and had helped to stone Stephen, was a Pharisee with a Greek education, so that to the Hebraic separation of God from man, and man from nature, he added Plato's division of all into reality and appearance, soul and body, this world and the next. But the mind of this fanatical convert was far from the golden mean of the Greeks, and Paul could only spread that disease of duality from which all the Christian centuries have since suffered. Eloquent on matters of ideal love, he could only allow to the body that 'it is better to marry than to burn' and to that end he called: 'Wives, submit yourselves to your husbands, as unto the Lord.'

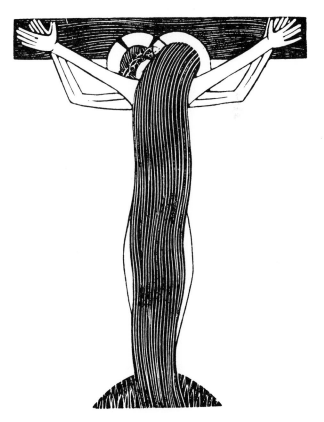

OPPOSITE. Jacob Epstein : *Madonna and Child*

Two women in the Bible have had a large part in shaping Christianity: one a whore, the other a mother. The first, Mary Magdalene, understandably became the beloved saint of many. She was a sinner as themselves, and yet Jesus was to say of her: 'Her sins, which are many, are forgiven for she loved much.' This assumes, however, that her sins were of the body only, and it has furthered the link of woman with the sin of lust. The Church could allow the sun to shine on Mary Magdalene only as a repentant sinner.

LEFT. *St Mary Magdalene*
BELOW. Leonardo da Vinci : *Study for the Virgin and Child with St Anne and St John the Baptist* (detail)

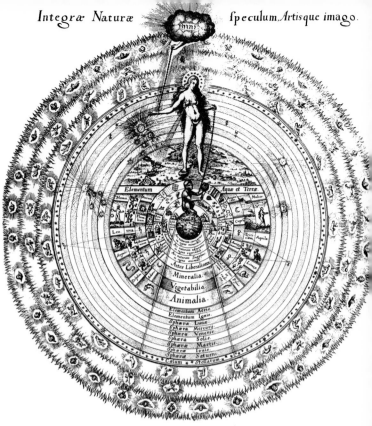

RIGHT. Woman as mediator between the invisible
Godhead and the manifest world

The other woman, Mary the mother of Jesus,
has little mention in the Bible but was to become
the primary shaping force of the Catholic
Church, even ousting for many the influence of
her son. Mary's elevation, in spite of scant mention of her in the scriptures, was brought about
by the insistent need for the Feminine in the
world of men, the same need that had given
worship to the Goddess in all her many guises
over the ages. In awareness of this, Constantine
ordered the destruction not only of all temples to
the Goddess, but also forbade worship of Mary,
lest it overwhelm due regard for her Son. It was
St Patrick's realization that the pagan world
would accept Christ only if his mother was
allowed to take the place of the Goddess that
changed the official attitude of the Church to
Mary. The fathers of the Church, in the interests
of survival, had to give way to the popular
demand for the Feminine mother: 'The mother
alone was human, imperfect, and could love . . .
The Mother alone could represent whatever was
not Unity; whatever was irregular, exception,
outlawed; and this was the whole human race.'[20]

RIGHT. Gregor Erhart : *The Madonna of Mercy*

The Church's acceptance of the Mother, as with that of the Whore, could, however, come only after she was freed of the stain of sex and made into a *Virgin* Mother — that wholly unnatural symbol of the Feminine. The ideal of a Mother who yet remained intact, *semper Virgo*, could be held in the minds of men together with all other ideals of purity, goodness, modesty and grace — ideals that do not disturb as does the love of ordinary women. Seeing 'something base and sinister in the female element', Nicholas Berdyaev insisted that: 'The cult of the Mother of God, of the Most Holy Virgin, is essentially distinct from pagan worship of female principle; it is worship of womanhood which is entirely illumined and serene, which has achieved victory over the base element in femaleness.'

LEFT & BELOW. Carlo Crivelli : details from *The Annunciation*

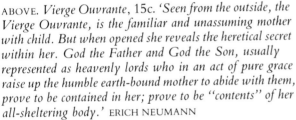

ABOVE. *Vierge Ouvrante*, 15c. *'Seen from the outside, the Vierge Ouvrante, is the familiar and unassuming mother with child. But when opened she reveals the heretical secret within her. God the Father and God the Son, usually represented as heavenly lords who in an act of pure grace raise up the humble earth-bound mother to abide with them, prove to be contained in her; prove to be "contents" of her all-sheltering body.'* ERICH NEUMANN

The strong and insistent worship of the Feminine by the masses finally put Mary among the men in heaven. In proclaiming the dogma of the Assumption, Pope Pius XII said that 'The place of the bride whom the Father had espoused was in the heavenly courts.' But as C.G. Jung pointed out: 'For more than a thousand years it has been taken for granted that the Mother of God dwelt there, and we know from the Old Testament that Sophia was with God before the Creation . . . it was recognized even in pre-historic times that the primordial divine being was both male and female. But such truth even-tuates in time only when it is solemnly pro-claimed or rediscovered. It is psychologically significant for our day that in the year 1950 the heavenly bride was united with the bride-groom.'[21]

The Church can only slowly come to accept alien elements, but the consequences of a woman in heaven must seem incalculable when her inclu-sion is properly seen also to include all that the minds of men have associated with women — matter itself, the earth, the body, sex, even evil.

47

The medieval attempt, however, to deny these other aspects by the elevation of the Most Holy Virgin, could only bring about her excessive opposite in the form of the Devil: 'The Mary-myths and the Devil-myth formed themselves side by side, neither possible without the other. Disbelief in either of them was a deadly sin . . . It was not only the love-glowing hymns to Mary, but the cries of countless pyres as well that rose up to heaven. Hard by the Cathedral were the gallows and the wheel.'[22]

The inevitable working of the opposites did not only show in these ways, and not only among the ignorant masses. Pope John XII in the tenth century kept women in the Vatican. Pope John XIII 'found nunneries as amusing to visit as brothels'. In 1211, a Franciscan monk, Brother Salimbene, found it necessary to warn his young niece of 'the common habit of confessors who take their little penitents behind the altar in order to copulate with them'. In the same century, when Pope Innocent IV left Lyon after ten years there, Cardinal Hugo said in his farewell speech to the citizens: 'We have made great improvement since we have been here. When we arrived, we found three or four brothels. We are leaving only one behind us. We must add, however, that this one brothel stretches from the east to the west gate.' When, in the fifteenth century, the Council of Basle met, fifteen hundred whores ministered to the needs of the fathers of the Church.

But not all virtuous men could in this way allow themselves the best of both worlds, embracing Venus at night and worshipping the Virgin Mary in the morning, as Pope Innocent III complained of his clergy. For some, the equation of celibacy with sanctity meant identifying woman with the Devil, the body and the burning world. Many who determined to be pure-minded even ceased to wash lest the sight of their own flesh gave way to what St Augustine called 'hell's black river of lust'. St Simeon, who was spoken of as a very angel on earth, the glory of Antioch and Syria, dropped vermin as he walked, and then got himself as far as possible from the impure world by climbing to the top of a high pillar to be the 'most holy martyr in the air'.

LEFT. Verner Klemke : *Monk and Nun*

48

Alas for him and the likes of him, the world, the flesh and the Devil rose after them into the air, went with them into the desert. It was clear to St Jerome that married people lived with one another 'like cattle', in no way different from 'pigs and irrational animals.'[23] How, he asked, could anyone find pleasure in a pretty, voluptuous girl; how could anyone sleep beside a death-dealing serpent?[24] But it was one thing to keep a pretty girl from one's bed, another to put her from one's mind. The same Jerome told: 'How often when I was living in the desert, in the vast solitude which gives to hermits a savage dwelling . . . how often did I fancy myself among the pleasures of Rome . . . When I had no companions but scorpions and wild beasts, I often found myself among bevies of girls. My face was pale and my frame chilled with fasting, yet my mind was burning with desire and the fires of lust kept bubbling up before me when my flesh was as good as dead.'[25]

RIGHT. *St Simeon the Stylite*

BELOW. Rosalind Dease, drawing

Saint Augustine at Thirty-Two

Girl, why do you follow me
When I come to the threshold of the holy place?
My resolution falters: it seems a death to enter
When, turning back, I look into your face.

I saw you when I lay alone
And ran from you as from a searching light
Into the gentle, acquiescent
Obscurity of the night.

I crave communion that is not words
And life fulfilled in my cell alone —
And you, you come with your lips and your gold
*   hair,*
And at your feet is a leaf that the wind has blown.

CLIFFORD DYMENT

49

Such attitudes did not die with the Dark Ages. They continued through all the centuries and continue even today — our obsessive society now shows only the inverse of those attitudes.

The Church fostered the belief that all sin was due to Eve and so to all women since; that while man was made in the image of God, woman was made for man's use. All the while, however, there were feminine elements also working within Christianity to soften the cruelties of the times. An early Church Council proclaimed that: 'A Christian husband is bound to chastise his wife *moderately*,' and the Bishop of Salisbury in the thirteenth century instructed nuns to 'wear no iron, nor haircloth, nor hedgehog skins; and do not beat yourselves therewith'. They had done all such things.

The Middle Ages approved only of nuns or wives, and since women were often forced to enter convents, the atmosphere in these grew lax. Chaucer's Prioress wore her cloak with grace and with a brooch emblazoned: *Love conquers all*. It allowed interpretations; she was most gentle of heart but not holy by ecclesiastical standards.

The romantic view of woman that derives from the inability to take her whole was to show in chivalry and in the worship given to inaccessible women, without any conscious thought of intimacy with them. Such idealization of women is the other side of their abuse, but it did work to make men more acquainted with gentleness, where they had only been gross; made for the emergence of the Woman within them, and so for greater regard for women in the world.

The Renaissance brought about a new world. In accordance with Christian ideals women had been required to do nothing but housework, to spin and weave, to assist and serve their husbands in all ways, as in bed. The new learning of the sixteenth century reached even women, at least those in privileged homes. Great scholars were ready to tutor the women of the rich and spoke of them as reasonable beings.

The Reformation, in allowing priests to marry, reformed the Church's attitude to marriage and brought women into active participation even in spiritual matters. 'Our very Reformation of Religion', wrote the governess of Elizabeth Stuart in the seventeenth century, 'seems to be begun and carried on by women.'

LEFT. *The Prioress.* Illustration to Chaucer's *Canterbury Tales*

With women's entry into the world of men came better homes and comforts, feather beds and fine linen, delight in dressing, in eating and drinking. The advent of Puritanism, however, not only brought this to an end but also renewed the persecution of women as witches. The healing of sickness had long been the province of women; by the same token, the outbreak of sickness was sometimes accredited to them. By the logic of man's reasoning, witchery could for certain be proved by a dip in a river: if the bound woman drowned, she was innocent; if she survived she was clearly a witch. 'You shall not allow a sorceress to live,' it had been said in Exodus. Such a woman was tied to a cross in a rat-infested dungeon or roasted over a slow fire. One woman was told: 'You are to be tortured so thin that the sun shall shine through you.'

LEFT. Hans Holbein : *Woman Walking*
BELOW. *Ordeal by water of Mary Sutton.* From a pamphlet entitled 'Witches Apprehended, Examined and Executed'

With the Restoration and the reaction to Puritanism, women of 'good position' became playthings again, lacking not only learning but also virtue. Little was asked of them: 'A woman in this age', said Hannah Wooley, 'is considered learned enough if she can distinguish her husband's bed from that of another.'

Natural virtue was to be found only in the country where Dorothy Osborne used to 'walk out on a common . . . where a great many young wenches keep sheep and cows, sitting in the shade and singing of Ballads . . . I talk to them and find they want nothing to make them the happiest people in the world but the knowledge that they are so.'

RIGHT. Edward Francis Burney : *An Elegant Establishment for Young Ladies* (detail)

LEFT. Thomas Rowlandson : *Landscape, Isle of Wight* (detail)

If the life of women in the country had not greatly altered, it was quickly changed by the Industrial Revolution. 'All our properties,' said William Cobbett, 'all our laws, all our manners, all our minds changed.' Women had worked long hours but at home and in healthy surroundings. Now it was found that 'their labour is cheaper and they are more easily induced to undergo severe body fatigue than men.'

Women went down the mines and according to Lord Shaftesbury 'always did the lifting or heavy part of the work, for females submit to work in places where no man or even lad could be got to labour in; they work in the bad roads, up to their knees in water, in a posture nearly double; they are below ground to the last hour of pregnancy.'

Things were more strait-laced among the rich women of the eighteenth-century towns whose daughters were sent to learn by ridiculous and sometimes cruel means how to deport themselves in order to gain husbands. In the mean streets, apart from these 'Elegant Establishments for Young Ladies', women died of childbirth, of overcrowding and lack of sanitation, if not of cheap gin.

In the homes of the upper classes, idleness meanwhile was a symbol of status. Servants were cheaply available to save such women from the labour of bringing up their own children, and with the ideal of woman's submission to man, there were many children in the Victorian nurseries.

With the second half of the nineteenth century, however, a new attitude slowly began to show. The seeds of women's liberation were sown in the mines and factories and in the homes of those women whose concern for their sisters led them into philanthrophy and into a growing realization of the crime so long committed against women: 'Why', asked one, 'have women passion, intellect, moral activity — these three — and a place in society where no one of them can be exercised?'

Inspired by the French and American revolutions, Mary Wollstonecraft at the close of the eighteenth century had called for women's 'equal rights'. But support was for long lacking in any political party. At the close of the nineteenth century, Mr Gladstone explained himself: 'I have too much respect to seek to trespass on the delicacy, the purity, the refinement, the elevation of women's nature to give them the vote.' At the beginning of the twentieth century, Mrs Pankhurst among others felt that only extreme measures could bring change about, and turned to civil disobedience. The Women's Suffrage movement was born.

It took a war, however, to bring some small change in men's attitudes. The campaign for suffrage was called off; women offered themselves in service to the country and showed themselves well able to stand at the side of men, or instead of them. There were also women of as much or more courage who opposed war, assisted conscientious objectors in prisons, as well as German women in England, and after the Armistice organized relief work in Germany in spite of the protests of more righteous men and women.

ABOVE. *Arrest of Mrs Pankhurst outside Buckingham Palace*

OPPOSITE RIGHT BELOW. *Woman dragging loaded cart in coal mine*
RIGHT. *First World War nurse in France*

With the Second World War confirming women's abilities, it seemed that their rights were assured. Patriarchal attitudes, however, persist in spite of all laws and changing circumstances; they persist in men who wish women well, and even now in women who insist on the liberation of women. We have lived so long under the domination of masculine values that we cannot know the meaning of women's liberation; it is told in masculine terms, in a masculine manner with violence, shouts, slogans, in all the old ways.

The militant *Women's Libber* can seem a tragic figure; not in the cause she espouses but in her way of expressing it. Her Feminism is directed not only against men but even against her own feminine nature. She shows an abject acceptance of masculine values in claiming the same right to them; she flatters by imitation. It is not simply that she 'doth protest too much', but that her protest reveals its roots in the lack of ease within her, the lack of feminine/masculine balance, with its inevitable extremism.

One speaker for *Women's Lib*, brought up in a convent, assumes that man's casual coupling is evidence of an enviable freedom and calls women to be 'deliberately promiscuous'. Love, she says, is a 'cognitive act', and bringing up children is 'not a real occupation, because children come up just the same, brought up or not'. She tells at the same time of her mother who once 'knelt on my

small brother's chest and beat his face with her fists . . . after nagging and badgering her eldest child into running away from home'.[26] Other protagonists explain that pregnancy is 'barbaric', giving birth is like 'shitting a pumpkin'; motherhood is only 'animal'.[27] There exists a Society for Cutting Up Men; its manifesto proclaims that 'SCUM will kill all men who are not in the men's auxilliary of SCUM'.[28]

The old imbalance in men, the inadequacy and inner conflict that has shown in aggression of all kinds, shows in such statements. There is the same patriarchal attitude to the animal body. That it should show in women is tragic.

The wish for revenge after centuries of exploitation is understandable. What is certain is that no good comes of revenge. *Women's Lib*, as all revolutions, can be seen as a symptom of the sickness of the society it is trying to change; it should not be confused with health.

ABOVE LEFT AND RIGHT. *Women police watching over demonstration for women's rights, New York,* 1972
OPPOSITE ABOVE. *Women's Liberation, London,* 1970
OPPOSITE BELOW. Paola Agosti : *Women's Liberation, Rome,* 1977. *'From now on we decide.'* A protest against male control by the way of the Church, the Medical Profession, the Law and big business.

See
That no matter what you have done
I am still here.
And it has made me dangerous, and wise.
And brother,
You cannot whore, perfume, and suppress
    me anymore.
I have my own business in this skin
And on this planet.

                                        GAIL MURRAY, 1970

ABOVE. Paola Agosti : *Women's Liberation, Rome,*
1977. 'At last we are women; no longer whores or
madonnas.' *The Women's Movement in Italy is unique:
more radical than elsewhere since repression there has been
greater; yet its demonstrations are without aggression; its
nature is not so much a protest as a joyous and creative
celebration; a movement not so much* against *men as* for
*women. Its greeting is a sign for the vulva held high in the
air.* From *Emma* magazine, Cologne

All that is good comes by growth, begins with
an awareness and acceptance of facts — the way of
the Feminine. From that first acceptance changes
can come. Manifestos are always framed in brave
words that conceal a fear of real change, avoid the
issue of changing oneself.

What the Feminine *is* cannot be formulated.
After centuries of masculine rule and reason, we
can have little or no idea of it. The Feminine is not
an idea; ideas are of the masculine mind. It is not
an ideal; ideals are masculine. It is not to be
achieved; achieving is a masculine impulse. The
Feminine can only be found, in women and in
men.

It is not that nothing can be done, but that
whatever is done will only be well done as an
expression of growth. Much needs to be done,
but it needs to be done by the right woman, the
right man. 'When the wrong man does the right
thing, the right thing works in the wrong way,'
said a Chinaman once and for all time. We have
suffered not only from wrong doing, but also
from centuries of wrong men meaning to do the
right thing, the ideal thing, with disastrous consequences.

The adolescent nature of *Women's Lib* is made
apparent by the call of some for a Matriarchal
Counter-Revolution to replace the old Patriarchal take-over. Our need now is not for Mother
or Father images that keep us as children, but for
an adulthood that does not deny its parents
because it is free of them; is freed thereby for
relationship with them as with others and all else
in the world.

The way to adulthood, in women as in men,
must lie in going from the confines of the parental
home to a meeting with all that seems strange and
other; for woman it is in her meeting with man in
the world; for man it is his meeting with woman.

OPPOSITE. Pablo Picasso : *Life*

56

The liberation of women, as that of men, can only lie in their coming to individual wholeness. This begins with a clear understanding of the difference between Feminine and Masculine ways; an understanding that does not lie in the mind apart but in one's meeting with what is opposite and seems other, in *experiencing* the difference. Experience of this brings a realization that what is outside us mirrors what is within, and reveals the need of inward marriage in the individual. The outcome of that inward marriage in each woman and each man will then manifest in the world in the right relationship of women and men, in creation of all kinds, and in peace, not as an ideal to be achieved but as a natural consequence of the harmony within.

'Only the recognition that the entire nature of woman is different from men, that it signifies a new vivifying principle in human life, makes the women's movement, in spite of the misconceptions of its enemies and its friends, a social revolution.'[29]

LEFT. *The Witches Sabbath*

That's why we become witches: to show our scorn of pretending life's a safe business, to satisfy our passion for adventure . . . to have a life of one's own, not an existence doled out to you by others.
SYLVIA TOWNSEND WARNER: *Lolly Willowes*

Towards the end of the twentieth century, we must seem far from that Mother Goddess of the beginning, and we are fast outgrowing the Father God who replaced her. Such images have already ceased to satisfy many for the need is in them, however unconsciously, to grow, to be adult and whole.

And yet in a world that is a timeless Whole — one in which all things grow in time — we can expect to find the present as a seed hidden in the past, the end in the beginning. It was there and it is here. The Feminine that was the Mother Goddess of all human and other kind, has since shown in all imaginable and unlikely guises, calling and compelling, luring and alarming: as Queen of Heaven and as Whore of All the World, as Virgin and as every mortal carnal woman here on earth. The Feminine shows also as *Sophia*, the very Spirit of God, and so as the essential heart of Everyman.

RIGHT & BELOW. Margaret Michaelis : *Bodenweiser Ballet*

Even in the language of the patriarchal Hebrews, the *shekinah*, the Spirit of God, was feminine. So also among the Greeks, the Wisdom of God was the feminine Sophia, his consort in the Bible who sings: 'The Lord possessed me in the beginning of his way, before his works of old. I was set up from everlasting, from the beginning, or ever the earth was . . . and I was daily his delight, rejoicing always before him; rejoicing in his habitable earth; and my delight was with the sons of men.'[30]

In ceasing to look out and up to the gods of old, we find their reality deep within us. We are not driven either to the idolatory of ideas and ideal beings or to a blind taking of the world, but are given to the spirit of things, little and large, above and below, within and without. That spirit is not 'spiritual', is not 'holy' but *whole*; it is 'the heart of things', to be known by heart and so not to be found apart from the love of things, not apart from the earth, nor from the bodies of women and men or the forms of animals, plants, rocks and planets; not apart from the whole body of the Universe, of all that is and all that is not.

59

REFERENCES

1. EMPEDOCLES, fifth century BC
2. *The Way of Life According To Laotzu* trs. Witter Bynner, G.P. Putnam's Sons, New York, 1944
3. WITTGENSTEIN, Ludwig: *Tractus Logico-Philosophicus* Routledge & Kegan Paul, London, 1962
4. The Enuma Elish, trs. William Muss-Arnholt, *Assyrian and Babylonian literature* quoted in GOULD-DAVIS, Elizabeth: *The First Sex* Penguin Books, London, 1975
5. *Brihandaranyaka Upanishad* 1.1V.
6. STEVENS, Wallace : *Collected Poems*, Faber & Faber, London, 1955
7. LORCA, Federico Garcia : 'Yerma' from *Lorca's Theatre, Five Plays of Federico Garcia Lorca* Scribners, New York, 1941
8. BACHOFEN, J.J. : *Myth, Religion and Mother Right* Princeton University Press, Princeton, New Jersey, 1973
9. GOULD-DAVIS, Elizabeth: *The First Sex*, reporting the findings of James Melaant, archaeologist in charge of first diggings at Catal Huyuk, 1961
10. GOULD-DAVIS, Elizabeth : *ibid*., quoting J.J. Bachofen
11. Maori creation myth, quoted in ERICH NEUMANN : *The Origins And History Of Consciousness* Routledge & Kegan Paul, London, 1954
12. CAMPBELL, Joseph : *The Masks of God : Occidental Mythology* Secker & Warburg, London, 1965
13. Deuteronomy 12.2
14. Joshua 10.40
15. Jeremiah 44.15-18
16. Jeremiah 6
17. Jeremiah 4.26
18. Lamentations 1-2
19. Jeremiah 31
20. ADAMS, Henry : *Mont Saint-Michel and Chartres* Doubleday, New York, 1959
21. JUNG, C.G. : *Answer to Job. The Collected Works of C.G.Jung* Volume II Routledge & Kegan Paul, London, 1958
22. SPENGLER, Oswald : *The Decline of the West* Allen & Unwin, London, 1961
23. KAHL, Joachim : *The Misery of Christianity* Penguin Books, London, 1971
24. HAYS, H.R. : *The Dangerous Sex* G.P. Putnam's Sons, New York, 1964
25. *ibid*.
26. GREER, Germaine : *The Female Eunuch* Paladin, London, 1971
27. FIRESTONE, Shulamith : *The Dialectic of Sex: The Case For Feminist Revolution* Jonathan Cape, London, 1971
28. SOLANAS, Valerie : Manifesto of SCUM, quoted in ARIANNA STASSINOPOULOS : *The Female Woman* Davis-Poynter, London, 1973
29. BRAUN, Lily : quoted in THEO LANG : *The Difference Between a Man and a Woman* Michael Joseph, London, 1971
30. Proverbs 8.22-31

ABOVE. *The Lovers*. Card from Marseille Tarot pack

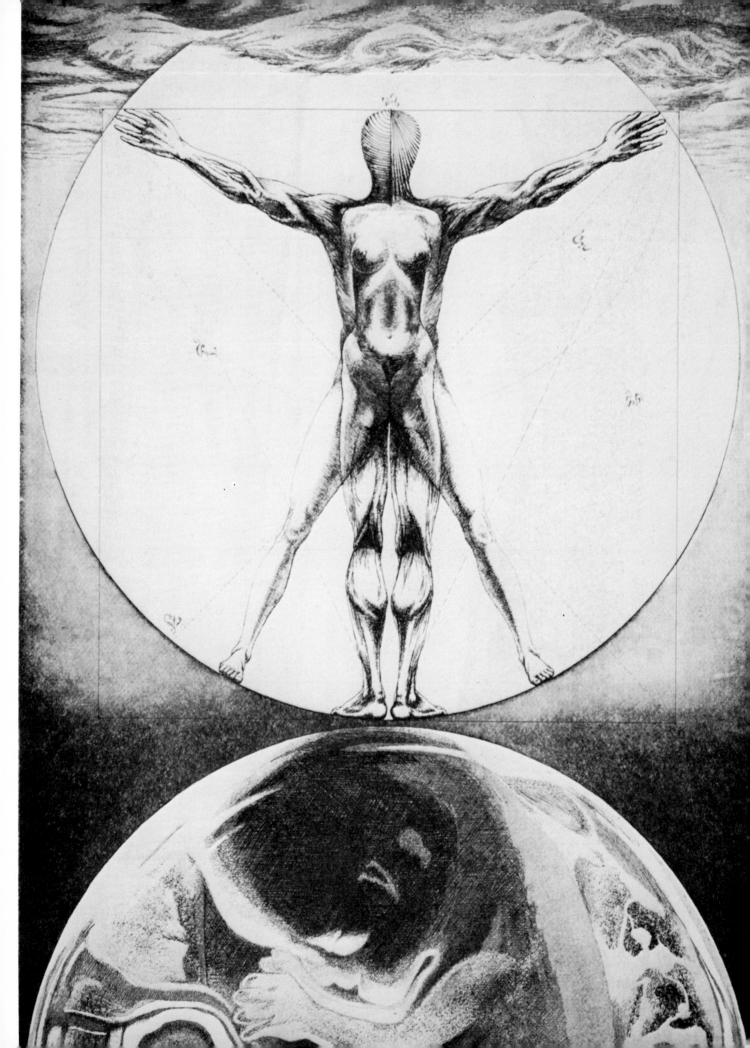

II *Woman Within*

The marvel is that I fled from Woman to this woman. A vertiginous journey: thought becomes incarnate, and I am in it and cannot conceive of a greater mystery.

LOUIS ARAGON

. . . not balances
That we achieve but balances that happen,
As a man and woman meet and love forthwith.
WALLACE STEVENS

It is fatal to be a man or a woman pure and simple; one must be a woman manly, or a man womanly.

VIRGINIA WOOLF

THREE YOUTHS WITH DOWN ON THEIR CHINS, dreaming to be mighty in bed as bearded Mormons of old, sat in a café and looked shyly, slyly on a painted woman alone at a table not far from them. Among the stories they told to shore up their manhood was an old one that may well have been told by their fathers' fathers to ease *their* ache after women and their anxiety. Born of the movement for women's rights earlier in the century, the story told of a militant feminist who ended her long tirade with the statement: 'After all, there's very little difference between men and women.' Whereupon a man at the back of the hall called out: 'Three cheers for the very little difference.'

The jest is at the expense of women and is stale, but — except when asserting the natural superiority of women — some *Women's Libbers* even today hold to the dogma of the 'very little difference'. Even today when it is a commonplace of biology that women and men differ at conception and are unalike in all their cells, and when the unity of body and mind is elementary knowledge, it has been asserted by one woman who would be liberated that 'the sexes are inherently in everything alike save reproductive systems, secondary sexual characteristics, orgasmic capacity, and genetic and morphological structure.'[1]

Are these not differences enough?

To assert that such differences are of no consequence is to be less than children who lift skirts and down trousers in a summer field:

My memory of the moment when I discovered that the body of my favourite playmate lacked such a tassel as my body possessed is vivid enough to have survived to this day with all its attendant details of scene and scent and sound; and I hold firmly to the opinion that she and I can be numbered among the lucky ones in that this sexual revelation burst upon us amid the clean sane beauty of a sunlit Yorkshire meadow during an interval between picking flowers. The girl found the difference so diverting that she curled up in giggles, but then, to mollify any affront to my pride such derision might have caused, she honoured my masculinity with a decoration of cowslips. All that, years before Lady Chatterley.[2]

OPPOSITE. Jaroslav Bradac : *The Sixth Day*

Such children may be unaware of the implications of their discovery, but do not deny them. With instinctive wisdom the girl celebrated the difference.

The very little difference makes a world of difference. It makes the world — the misery and the magnificence of it. Some of the misery has been told and still shows in our times; much of the magnificence is still to be found.

It will be found when the true difference between women and men is realized, for only then will it be seen in what respects they are alike, and so may come together to bring about a common end.

The little difference between a woman and a man is more than enough; it is even wanton and prodigal since sex is quite unnecessary. For two-thirds of the earth's existence there was reproduction without sex. Life very capably increased by the simple though miraculous process of multiplication by division, the splitting of one basic form into two. So there are today such simple forms of amoeba, fungae, parmacea, even sea squirts which, it seems, are 'about the most complicated thing that can reproduce by dividing.'[3] There is no shortage of sea squirts.

But if by life is meant more than mere numerical increase; if more life means greater liveliness; if it means magnificence, then something else is needed.

> . . . to equal a need
> Is natural, animal, mineral: but to fling
> Rainbows over the rain
> And beauty above the moon, and secret rainbows
> On the domes of deep sea-shells
> And make the necessary embrace of breeding
> Beautiful also as fire
> Not even the weeds to multiply without blossom
> Nor the birds without music:
> There is the great humaneness at the heart of
> things
> The extravagent kindness, the fountain . . .[4]

If there are to be dragonflies and seals, coral snakes, birds of Paradise and grey lumbering elephants, women and men, then sex is necessary. And there are not women and men simply, but those who dream and dare and do all manner of things, who laugh and weep, hold one another or go alone, are silent sometimes, sometimes still, so living in their own way and, in life's way, one day dying. For all the enriching sorrows and splendours of humankind, the very little difference is essential, between them and in them both.

ABOVE & OPPOSITE. Sandra Hovas : *Children in a Texan landscape*

'I would make a pilgrimage to the deserts of Arabia,' cried Coleridge, 'to find the man who could make me understand how the one can be many.' The one is many by becoming two; these two being different from one another and apart as the poles of the earth. As those poles, they are of a Whole, and as those poles, the two attract one another. The rest follows. But that the one can be many is a half-truth; the other half is that the many can be one.

Stripped in a sunlit meadow a girl and a boy gaze upon one another's nakedness and so discover the open secret of the universe. The difference between them is cosmic. The one energy that flows through them flows through all the phenomena of the world and in the same way: in two apparently opposite directions. There seems to be nothing *or* something, death *or* life, darkness *or* light, stillness *or* movement, feminine *or* masculine, girl *or* boy.

The difference between girl and boy is clear, though it may seem small at the start: a cleft between the thighs of the girl, a tassel on the boy. But with their growing the difference grows: the cleft will seem to open on to an abyss as the girl ripens and bears fruit; small apples swell and soften into breasts, her hips add flesh and widen so that she walks at her best slow and sure and swaying, already weighted by the future and showing in the way she is made that for which she is made: not for the bearing of children only —that may or may not happen — but to bring into the world the way of complementary opposites and so the possibility of creation of all kinds by her readiness to receive, her ability to contain, to nourish, to tend, to inspire and so to transform and bring about. By that small cleft between her thighs, the girl is already marked for the part she will play, as for the way that she will incline to play it.

The shape of things reveals their essential nature. A cave is not simply an aspect of landscape; it is of the nature of the Feminine and so is secret and fraught in a way that an upright stone is not. With that dark cave between her thighs, a woman will have an awareness of Space in a measure not always at the start given to a man: 'In the last resort,' said C.G. Jung, 'the void is a great feminine secret. For man it is something utterly alien, the yawning gulf of otherness, the yin.'

The small boy, meanwhile for his part grows broad about the shoulders, gets slim muscled hips, and his limp tassel may now at the sight of a girl stiffen and thrust into the space that is outside him, being drawn to the space within the girl. Given these signs of his body, it is not surprising that the boy in becoming a man shows more of will than of willingness; with the balance of his weight set about his shoulders, higher than a woman's, he will have less stability and more

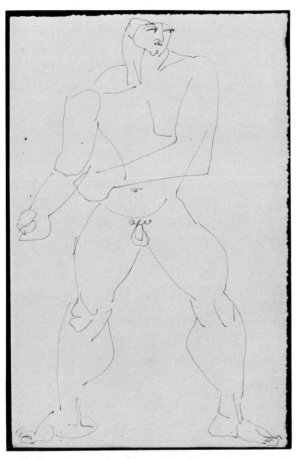

mobility; instead of creating by quiet containment will spill over into outward activity, to recreate the world about him.

There is nothing here of superiority or inferiority; nothing in itself good or bad, better or worse. These differences are differences, simply.

OPPOSITE ABOVE. Russell Lee : *Girl and boy,* Italy
OPPOSITE BELOW. Augustus John : *Artist's Children*
ABOVE LEFT & RIGHT. Henri Gaudier-Brzeska : *Wrestler*
and *Standing Nude*
RIGHT. Russell Lee : *Lovers,* Italy

A woman does not 'lack a tassel'. It took a masculine mind to conceive that a woman might suffer from 'penis envy', and a *Women's Lib* movement, masculine in spirit, to seem to prove the man right. A woman's body lacks nothing; it makes the most positive contribution to the meeting with a man's body. There can be no real conflict between women and men since their bodies are so clearly shaped to fit and come together. That vagina and phallus have need of one another is the natural need of opposites for one another. Difference attracts. Sameness repels. Conflict only arises when the same things make the same assertion, refusing to allow one another — as positive and positive, phallus and phallus, sword and sword. War is a 'masculine' occupation.

Opposite in appearance, vagina and phallus are for that reason complementary and without opposition, as are all feminine and masculine attributes. They are equal in all ways because they are in all ways different — in all ways but one: they are both partial and so need one another for that wholeness to which they both tend.

The difference between the opposites is clear. It is as clear that they are essentially of the same nature, since any one tendency taken to its extreme invariably changes into its opposite: the summit of a hill is the start of a valley; at the valley bottom the hill begins.

This interdependence and alternation of opposites shows through all the natural processes of the world: the sea ebbs and flows, night gives way to day, decay to growth; then flow and day

and growth make way for ebbing again, another night, further decay. The world is a Whole that now breathes in, now breathes out. The Whole is not one or the other; it is the interplay of both, the one *breathing*.

Life is not breath, for to have breath and hold it brings certain death. Life is the gain *and* the loss of breath. A game implies two players taking opposite sides, giving and taking; and the life of the game depends on no one winning. The defeat of any one player is the end of the game for both.

Barbara Whitehead, woodcuts

The language of play will seem paradoxical, even impossible to the mind which is linear, logical, and which purposefully aims to achieve its ends. Life has no purpose, no aim, no end. Logic cannot allow what is illogical, so that men may well be right when they accuse women of a lack of logic. Life is illogical. Being so, it can, illogically, include logic as it includes all else. Being whole, it will logically do so.

Life makes no sense, it has been said; it makes us, and makes us different: feminine and masculine. In that difference lies all delight and the means to further making. The creative artist, while he creates, experiences this: drawing upon the Feminine within for impulse and content, leaning upon the Masculine for the ordering and shaping of the given material.

To draw a straight line, sex is unnecessary. A man needs a ruler, a pencil, some paper, a steady hand. So in matters of purely linear logical thought (if there can be anything 'pure' — a purely 'masculine' conception), a man has mind enough. To add one to one and make two is also masculine, mathematical, simple.

But to imagine and make a whole painting, it is not enough to be man only. To do more than simplest arithmetic, to add one to one and make three or more, going beyond logic to life, a woman is needed, sex is necessary. And the answer will not be a tidy predictable sum but insurgent lawless life; the bawl and lively mess of a babe.

We have no means of telling of the One-that-is-many, nor of the way of it, for we have as yet little awareness of it. For so long our word for what is most real to us has been a noun, *God*; a male name, moreover, patriarchal and therefore partial, fixed and final. If we still hold to it, what shall we make of the living processes that modern science reveals as the very heart of things?

The old Chinese had a word for it, while insisting that there was no word for it: 'The *Tao* that can be told is not the *Tao*.' This *Tao* was not, as our God, set high and apart from the many things; it manifested as them, and in two ways, *Yin* and *Yang*, opposite and therefore complementary. These were, and are, in no way fast set and eternal but eternally changing in relationship one to the other, so that the *Tao* which is then both is itself endlessly transforming, is at every moment in everything more or less *Yin* or *Yang*. All things all the while change, for the nature of reality is Change.

But the way of things is not the way of them in China only, or only once upon a time; it is everywhere and always, here and now.

We need not then look to the East for wisdom but stand in our own back gardens, walk under our own skies upon our own hills, and regard one

ABOVE. *Yin-Yang*. Chinese symbol showing the dual nature of the one Tao. Dark/light, Female/male, as all other opposites are interdependent and contain one another. No one part can exist without its complementary opposite, or the whole interaction and play, the *life* of the Whole would be lost. The two balanced powers together make an all-embracing circle of unity.

BELOW. Felix Hoffmann : *Lovers*

another: the woman or the man before us. And if we want words we have them here in *Feminine* and *Masculine*, so long as we do not mean by these only sex — unless by sex we mean the differences in the natures of all things and the relationship between them. Indeed, it becomes essential that sex should be seen in this way, not genital but universal. We might then see, as the ancients did, a feminine earth under a masculine sun, a feminine sea encircling a masculine rock, a feminine valley giving rise to a masculine hill, and in this way of seeing we might recover, together with our regard for the Feminine and so for woman in the world and within us, some of the regard of pagan peoples for the earth they walked on in awe and trust and gratitude.

And for that which is the lively interplay of Feminine and Masculine, we already have a word that cannot be fixed or exclusively identified with either one or the other, nor set in the skies apart; it is in us and about us all the while, here and now in the living and dying of the many things — the one *Life*.

ABOVE. Fourteenth-century alchemical painting showing the Sun and the Moon, male and female, in opposition, yet each bears the sign of the other : the female carries the Sun on her shield; the male carries the Moon

The one Life takes the opposite shapes of valley and high hill, as of the two different tendencies that are here called Feminine and Masculine. All things, all qualities may be listed left and right, as two sides of one whole:

Feminine / Masculine
Invisible / Visible
Chaos / Order
Space / Time
Body / Mind
Instinct / Intellect
Acceptance / Assertion

These, as all other natural opposites, go together as in / out, as front / back. There cannot be one without its counterpart in greater or lesser measure. The play between them makes the game of life possible; the difference allows the dance. The very existence of one depends wholly on the other, as existence itself depends on non-existence: the shape and substance of any thing can be seen only because of the nothingness that surrounds it, the space that goes with it.

The whole way of Life can be seen in the working of any one pair of opposites. Weakness and strength, for example, can seem wholly opposed. Weakness is on the side of the Feminine, of acceptance and receptivity. Strength, being Masculine, tends to assertion and resistance; but strength carried to its extreme and to the attempted exclusion of weakness, brings weakness about, as the unbending oak branch under the burden of snow. The strong branch breaks and shows its weakness. The willow, meanwhile, weakly bends and by shedding the snow and surviving shows its strength. Strong and resistant forms of life have vanished from the earth while the weakness of man allows him to admit to the greater strength of outside forces; not to resist them and so be destroyed, but to see, to understand, to adapt, transform and survive.

As Life itself, so liveliness depends upon the opposites. Life is a Whole of differing, interdependent opposites in relationship and play with one another. The mind as we have come to know it, however, is masculine and partial, and therefore incapable of play. The mind of man is not content to see differences; it must divide. In taking thought without its opposite, man has torn the world in two: 'The essence of the conscious mind is discrimination; it must, if it is to be aware of things, separate opposites, and it does this *contra naturam* (against nature). In nature the opposites seek one another . . . and so it is in the unconscious.'[5]

This is not all, for the mind is not content to divide; it commends and condemns, taking sides not as in a game but as in war. The mind imagines 'good' and 'evil' — opposites not found in nature — and since assertion is the very existence of the masculine mind, it must assert all that can seem to contribute to its existence, naming it 'good', while denying all that seems to threaten, naming it 'evil'. With natural differences twisted into moral distinctions, the opposites are set in opposition, made enemies bent upon each other's defeat, no longer partners balancing one another. No longer do they come and go together as night and day, as winter and summer to make the whole round of the year.

OPPOSITE. Samuel Palmer : *A Hilly Scene*
RIGHT. *Zodiac*

73

There is no 'evil' but excess. The extreme assertion of any one opposite is 'bad' because it makes for imbalance; it is not a moral matter but a simple fact. Assertion of one opposite and denial of the other makes for 'evil' as for 'good'. Together the opposites have no more moral value than the negative and positive poles of electricity that are essential to one another for the making of a third thing that is new and other than either one of them alone, yet it is brought about by both.

The language of men does not describe things, it judges them. It is as though a tightrope walker who goes with grace and ease by spreading his arms wide and balancing by way of them, now dipping to the left a little, now to the right, determined instead to elevate one hand only and walk upright. If he is not to fall, however, that one hand must lower and the other rise up. So the extreme puritan's daily striving towards light and purity is balanced at night by dreams of dark women, even of the Devil — for some these are the same. We shall not come to live at ease until our language speaks of the opposites without fear or favour of one or the other. When we can speak of weakness and strength as two equal and essential forces, without praise or blame for either, we will then see women and men as equal, necessarily and delightfully different.

Light and law are meanwhile ranged with the mind on the side of the 'good' and so to be upheld at all costs, even at the expense of Life, while dark and chaos are aligned on the side of 'evil' and are denied. In putting the Feminine together with darkness and chaos on the side of evil, the 'masculine' mind has for two thousand and more years judged woman — in the world and within.

Out of the need to mature, to be adult and whole and not at the mercy of outward circumstance or inward impulse, mankind has grown a mind, that rich flowering of the body whose complexity and capacities we have begun, with the aid of that mind, to realize.

The mind has, however, grown to excess, to assert the part that it is as a whole in itself; it is 'masculine' in this. The difference between feminine and masculine that shows in the bodies of women and men, appears also in the minds of both. The mind, as all else, works in two ways: with wide feminine awareness or with narrow masculine attention.

Both are needed. The two ways are not in opposition; each is true to its time and place. A man may walk without thought in bright silent awareness of all that is about him, without any idea in his head that he is apart from all that surrounds him, from the cliff path he walks, the sea below him, the sky above, the gull in the air, the flower at his foot. He may then bend to look at the flower, withdrawing his awareness from the Whole to attend to the part. He may go further: first wondering on the flower he may then think upon it, distinguish it from all that is around it, even from other flowers, classifying it or only finding words to describe it, so bringing memory and knowledge, all that is of the past to the present of this one flower.

It is not wrongly done. It is the masculine and partial use of the mind, and well enough so long as the flower is seen as a part of the Whole, even as the act of close attention is. But while focussing on the flower, the *feel* of the flower tends to be lost; the sense of what that flower is may be lost, as may be the realization of its relationship to all about it, to earth and sky and him who sees it. When attention is no longer given to the flower alone, awareness of the living Whole may return.

OPPOSITE. Henry Moore : *Memorial Figure, Dartington Hall* (detail) Photo : Caroline Wyndham

75

The mind in its place as a part of the Whole plays its proper role. The part is not a fact in itself in opposition to the Whole. The Whole *is*, and the assertion of the part alone is a distortion of that fact.

Far from denying intellect, there is need of its full and free use undistorted by partiality, by values loftily imposed, which arise out of an imbalance in the whole being of a woman or a man.

The narrow attention of the masculine aspect of mind wedded to the wider awareness of the feminine aspect will not only focus on one minute particular but also relate it to all other such particulars, and all within an unknowable yet certain Whole. Intellect then ceases to be a dry stick that prods and probes, a knife that separates; it becomes a bright wand, becomes intelligence that brings things about without needing to know how.

This is not an achievement reserved for mankind; it shows in the least of creatures as that instinct which allows the miracles of migration.

In mankind the same wonder can manifest itself in a way appropriate to his being as a creature who may also have a part in creation.

As with all things, then, the masculine mind has need of its feminine opposite, its other half. But the other half of the mind is silence, is space, all that the masculine mind is not, and since the very 'masculinity' of the mind seems to lie in its self-assertion, it cannot easily lend itself to what seems a denial of itself. *I think, therefore I am*, said Descartes. Not to think must therefore seem not to be at all.

The masculine mind *is* its thoughts. But thoughts come and go and so, to secure permanence for itself, the mind separates itself from its transient thoughts and imagines an ego, sets up a centre it calls 'I', a fixed entity made up of memories that seem to remain all the while its thoughts come and go. Holding to the illusion of the 'I', the mind gains permanence and extension beyond all natural bounds. Thoughts die, but the 'I' does not. Being unreal it does not exist; is not born and does not die. The body knows sickness, but the 'I' can escape decay by denying its oneness with the body and by imagining an immortal spirit, a Self with which it identifies. The 'I' can escape into a still centre, find a way out of the turning world by becoming free of it, becoming 'enlightened'. The body must die but the 'I' can rise up to heaven, attain nirvana. All that is real, is whole and alive is certain to die, since death is its other half, but to illusion all things are possible, even life everlasting.

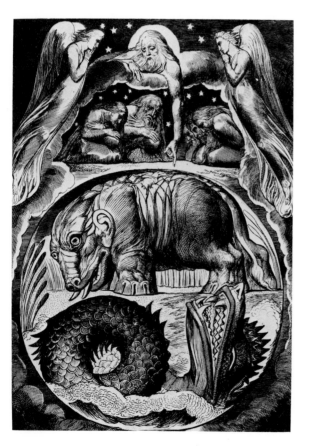

LEFT. William Blake : Illustration to *The Book of Job. Behold now Behemoth which I made with thee . . . Of Behemoth he saith, He is the chief of the ways of God* OPPOSITE. Henri Rousseau : *The Dream*, 1910

76

The assertion of the 'I', however, inevitably casts an accompanying shadow. Man's fear of woman is his fear of death, of darkness, of that chaos he is certain will overwhelm him if he does not hold to the light of his mind, to purity, to reason and the rule of law. The fear is revealed in legends as in bar-room jokes, in nightmares and in noble aspirations, in the prayers of the pious and the suffering of saints, in pornography as in those puritans who vehemently oppose it, and now in the alarm of some elders of the Church at the possibility of priestesses, as in ancient times.

The fear is old and it is understandable. In the long view of life, we are told, it is only a little while since humankind climbed out of the sea and slime of its infancy on earth; it is but a moment since the mind grew out of the dark matter of nature, away from the blind obedience to instinct, the realm of the Great Mother. The fear remains in man that he might turn back, might sink down again as the longing to do so is also in him, to be saved from the loneliness of adolescence, the challenge of adult consciousness.

ABOVE. Cyril Satorsky : *Rabbi Leib and the Female Demon, 1970. Rabbi Leib, in his youth, while visiting the secret city of Eblis, fell in love with a female demon. Years later he would try to recapture those sweet precious memories by having his wife pelt him with gobs of sweet and sour cabbage, gefilte fish, bacon rinds, and intricately carved mezuzahs till he screamed with delight. But it wasn't the same.*

The patriarchal age, for all its perversities, was a historical necessity, a need of the times. Out of dark and blind beginnings, man's consciousness is as a flower lifting from the mud in which it remains deeply rooted. The religions have in time played their necessary part: the *'rough beast, its hour come round at last / Slouches towards Bethlehem to be born.'*[6] Christianity offered a guiding light in the darkness, a Fatherly hand when the need arose to quit the safe enclosure of the Mother. The 'I' grew out of the same need for independence, and God the Father was therefore made in the image of man's ego, an Ultimate Ego, set apart from the chaos and seen as a male monarch with absolute enduring authority, enthroned high and alone, without any woman, queen or consort at his side to question him.

The being of the Cretan Goddess was her body: *I have breasts. I am.* It was not a thought in the mind. Woman remains close to the body and to the earth; a reminder to man of his roots and origin, and so of an essential part of his nature. Obeying laws that are not man-made or in any way subject to him, woman lives under the sway of the moon; red tides flow in her, from her; moods as unruly as the winds sweep over her; as a mother she is deep in the mire of the world, handling with sublime indifference, even with laughter, the piss and shit of her child, all that from which man would prefer to avert his eyes, his nose and mind, turning from all the dirt and disturbances of earthly life, to 'higher things'.

But the way of the opposites does not allow higher without lower, nor light without dark. So to the excessive brightness of a man's mind a woman offers necessary night. Mindlessly, man accepts and goes down to drown at her calling: *'Come on . . . don't be afraid . . . I'm moist . . . my necklace is made of mud, my breasts are dissolving, my pelvis is wet. I've got water in my crevasses, I'm sinking down . . . In my belly there are pools, swamps . . . There's moss . . . big flies, cockroaches, sowbugs, toads. Under the wet covers, they make love . . . they're swollen with happiness! . . . My mouth trickles down, my legs trickle, everything trickles down, runs, everything trickles, the sky trickles down, the stars run, trickle down, trickle . . .'*[7]

So, by way of woman, chaos is come again, as it must come again and again to those who would have their lives under the strict control of the mind, of morals or authority of any kind. Chaos must come since Life must be, that wholeness which is the most deep, most natural need of all women and all men. To insist on one opposite only — on either chaos or control — brings a lack of the other, which then asserts itself in the same measure as that first insistence.

OPPOSITE. Auguste Rodin : *Nude with Serpent*

78

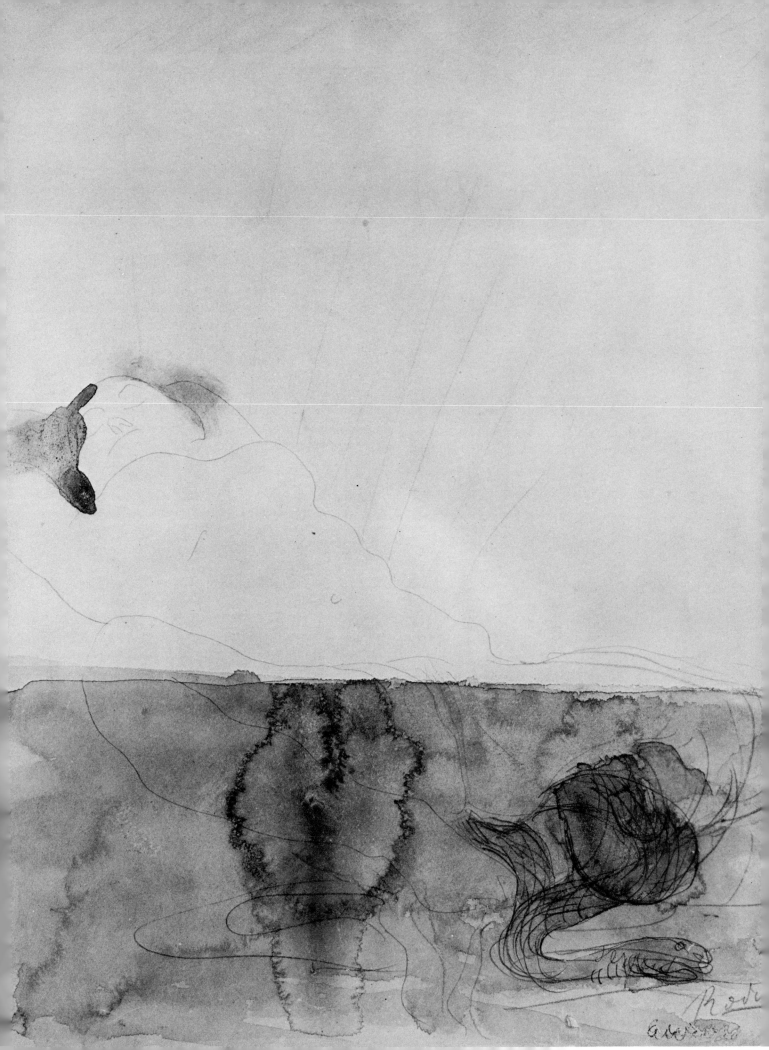

The assertion of God gives rise to the Devil. What we turn from climbs on our backs. The saint's insistent chastity casts a dark and comely shadow. Philosophers and scholars come down from their ivory towers, out of their brown studies into the beds of 'dumb blondes' so to save themselves from dehydration. In terror of the wasteland to which their thoughts bring them, men of brilliant intellect turn back to blind belief, in obedience to Mother Church. Sober respectable citizens, after a lifetime of acquiescence, break bounds before it should seem too late and they should lie on their death beds wondering what they had missed. Men of biggest business may for a while put aside their cunning ways for sight and respite of a stripped girl: Susannah upon a stage in Soho, naked as a daisy.

To save themselves from the excesses of their being, to keep themselves whole and somewhat sane, men must call up the dark to balance the excesses of mind and spirit. One can be destroyed by too much light as by an overwhelming darkness. Too much light too soon is the story of modern science and technology. Unbalanced men now juggle with balls of nuclear light.

It is not simply a matter of the control of dangerous powers. Control means division within— one 'sane' part of the mind may seek to hold in check its opposing insane part. But sanity of this kind and insanity make for one another. Wholeness is the marriage of opposites. Chaos without control is only destructive; control without chaos is only rigid and deathly. Together, they make for a lively ordering that is neither chaos nor control, but as the outcome of a marriage, a new being, a new way.

Robert Wyss : *Soho*

Women and men, we suffer one thing only — the lack of wholeness. Anything else we may seem to suffer is but another name for this lack; at most a symptom of it. The whole woman and the whole man will surely know the pain that is a part of Life, but they will not 'suffer' it. It is painful, simply, and they are deeply pained. Suffering is the refusal of pain, and is brought by the insistence on pleasure alone, by the wish to be without the pain that goes with pleasure.

In a world the way it is, the answer is to be *and* not to be. Given both pleasure *and* pain, the ability to smile *and* to weep, we already have all that is needed for that abundant life we seem to lack, the wholeness we seem to need. Wholeness is not as the offerings of religion, not Nirvana or high Heaven or Kingdom Come, not an ideal for the future but a present fact, as much as the fact of our two feet, the right and the left. Wholeness is to walk upon the earth at ease with ourselves and all about us. Given two feet and all else with them, we are already whole. The world, all the sorrowful joy of it, is also given; it remains for us to walk in it with sorrow and with joy.

One does not walk by standing upon one leg or the other, nor by standing on both legs, still and upright. Walking is not a fine point of balance carefully maintained between two opposite feet. It is, on the contrary, the careless ability to lean now to the left, now to the right; losing one's balance and regaining it, only to lose it again and have it again, so to keep moving. In Nietzsche's lofty words, 'We have all been summoned to become Cosmic Dancers who do not rest heavily on any one spot, but lightly turn and move from one position to another.'

RIGHT. Soho, 1975

But we are not summoned from above, nor called to do extraordinary dances. It is enough to walk, and to walk upon the earth in all seasons is more than enough. The body has all it needs for this, including a mind; it is only misdirected by the wrong and excessive use of the partial masculine mind. A liar does not walk as a man in love and so going lightly. The liar has two feet even as the lover, so that his limp is not in his limbs but in his mind. His whole body, however, limps since mind is of the body as surely as the feet. We have all that is needed for free and easy walking; it remains for us to remove impediments in us, the lies and illusions that make us limp.

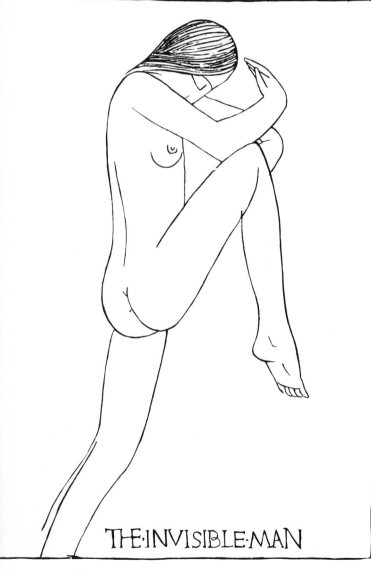

THE·INVISIBLE·MAN

It is a lie that we need anything in order to walk, an illusion that we are not already whole. Wholeness is not a final state to be achieved one day; as with walking, human wholeness is the living interplay at every moment of feminine and masculine in us. It is not a matter of either / or, but only of more or less at any moment. A woman when she leans forward to speak is being for the moment more masculine, less feminine; when she leans back to listen, the same woman is for that while being more feminine, less masculine. And if she should lean forward to listen and lean back to speak, she is in that an admixture of both feminine and masculine. And so it is with a man, exactly so. The measures of feminine and masculine in each woman and man differ every moment as they respond to circumstance and mood, to one another. The meeting of a woman and a man is at very least a meeting of four persons, all capable of playing infinite and interchangeable parts.

That a woman is, however, more disposed to all that is feminine, and a man to all that is masculine, is both factual and natural. The difference in disposition added to the differences in their bodies makes for lively marriage between them, for union and the outcome of children; even as the double nature within each of them makes for individual wholeness and creativity of all kinds. As walking is the interplay of the left foot and the right, so individual wholeness is the loving interplay of feminine and masculine, the harmony of inward marriage.

> . . . the intense yearning which each of them has for the other does not appear to be the desire of lovers' intercourse, but of something else which the soul of either evidently desires and cannot tell, and of which she has only a dark and doubtful presentiment . . . so ancient is the desire of one another which is implanted within us, reuniting our original nature, making one of two, and healing the state of man.
>
> PLATO

ABOVE. Edward Calvert : *The Chamber Idyll*
RIGHT. Charles Roff : *Lovers*
OPPOSITE LEFT. Eric Gill : *The Invisible Man*
OPPOSITE RIGHT. Eric Gill : *Artist and Mirror 1*

As with our feet, the feminine and the masculine in us is a given fact. To this extent, in the words of an old language: 'Marriages are made in heaven.' From the start of ourselves, side by side, there are two aspects in us, for better and worse, for richer and poorer, in sickness and in health, in all ways, inescapably, indissolubly, until death dissolves us. We may quarrel with ourselves, split and suffer estrangement; one part may think to dominate or deny the other, but what is done to one part is done to both, is suffered by the whole woman and man. Divorce is not possible within us. Upon the understanding of this inward marriage lies the possibility of harmony both in and between women and men.

And here, as in other more obvious ways, the need is for the liberation of Woman, of the Feminine in us. Our natures have overlong been dominated by the 'masculine' and its manifestation as the assertive mind in us. Understanding is the way of the Feminine in us. The Feminine lies under, underlies and so is the strong base of all that may be built, the deep root of all that will grow. The masculine, as man and as the rational mind in us, stands over and apart; it knows. It is no longer enough to know. Knowledge is needed and in no way to be denied; it may add to understanding, but understanding is not addition; it is a new thing; it happens; it is whole and involves the whole of ourselves.

Not understanding only, but marriage itself is also the way of the feminine. Marriage has been made on earth by woman and has been learned from her by man. In his mind as in his being, man is inclined to roam, to halt a while, touch and go. Woman, being touched, is made to stay, to make out of herself a secure and enduring shelter for the new life begun in her by man's momentary touch.

While an awareness of inward marriage is the common need of both women and men, they will come upon it differently because of the differences in their beings, their bodies, their beginnings.

Even before birth, in the very beginning, the way of conception can suggest different ways of adult perception:

The egg cell or female gamete, slow-moving, placid, enduring, receptive, occupies itself with accumulation and storage of food and libido for the ultimate purpose of creation — in a word, introverted; and the male gamete, active, impetuous, courageously self-sacrificing, with no reserves, resistive in the extreme, bent on forcing its personality and its body substance on the waiting ovum, possessing all those characteristics of the amoeba which are for action upon the outer world — in a word, extraverted.[8]

These descriptions of female and male are not, however, descriptions of women and men but of their inclinations, their tendencies. They are descriptions of the two aspects of each woman and each man.

Sex equality is no myth, for we are each of us essentially whole. It does not matter how deeply below a complete surface femininity we have to dig, there we find a complete male striving for expression. It does not matter how far down in the depth of the psyche we have to probe to find the woman in the painfully self-assertive male, there is the other half of the psyche in its entirety seeking for outlet and finding it by many strange paths.[9]

We are equal and different, being either female or male, and this difference will be stressed from the start and will increase. Born of woman, an infant girl comes of her own kind. The pain of leaving the wholeness of the womb is soon eased by her ability to identify with her mother, to gain strength and meaning from this. She grows and comes to know that she has a part to play in the scheme of things; her own mother shows it and (it is to be hoped) provides an example for her. What is done for her by her mother she will one day do for another, so that she can seem part of a process that reaches beyond the small moment of her individual being, beyond the being of her immediate mother, of her mother's mother, back into an immensity of mothers, even, however dimly sensed, to the Great Mother of all things. She reaches not only back in this way but forward too, since by giving birth and herself furthering Life one day, she will reach into the future, create that future. Taking her place in time can therefore bring her a sense of timelessness, of an eternity in which she can share by playing the part to which her body and instinctual being point.

OPPOSITE. John Christoforou : *Lovers*

RIGHT. *Birth Day*

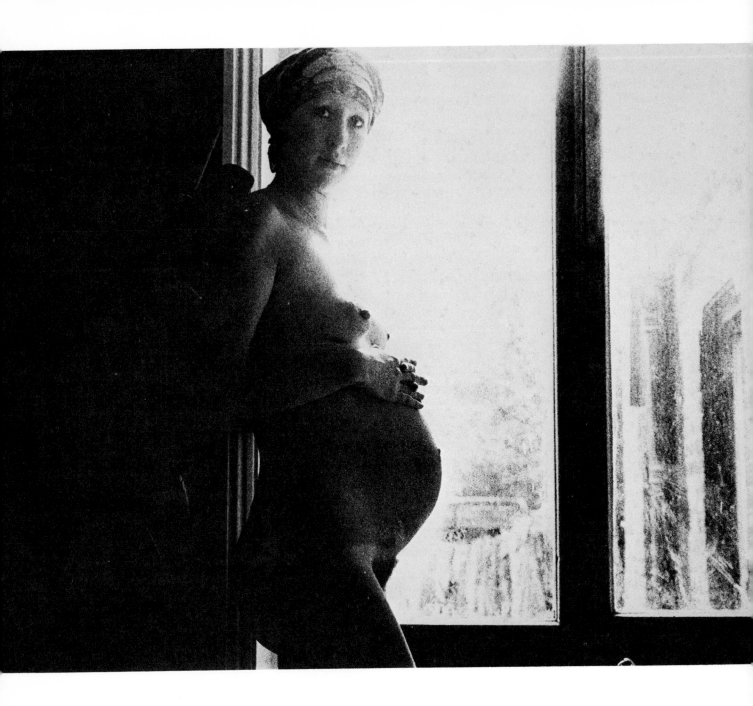

Nor will the girl seem a stranger to space; increasingly she becomes aware that it is within her. Her body will become as an empty stage where Life will assume new forms, find a new part to play. Moreover, in the space outside her it is the same, for there too she sees the female of all the species play the same part — beast and bird and flower, even the earth; even the universe is as a cornucopia at once empty and abundant; abundant *because* empty of itself.

But if the growing woman comes in this way to understand that the meaning of her life lies beyond what is only personal, she will, being feminine, as surely know that it can only come about by way of what is at once personal and particular. Those abstractions that come so easily to the minds of men are alien to her; she asks embodiment always, so that as she grows she calls for the body and being of a man in order that the meaning of her own being on earth as a woman may be given flesh and be made substantial.

86

A Husband's Song

When I see you, your fair head in a tissue of
    sunlight,
Standing at the back door discussing bread with a
    tradesman,
The garden beyond with its marshalled carrots
    and lettuce,
My heart turns in its cage where it has been
    pacing,
Lies, stretches, yawns and rests.
The voice of your singing fills all the nursery
Like a warm tongue, a child that cries
In the night cries
For the white moorland of your unceasing
    breasts.

You assume all complications and concern.
So many reins in your hand: from the high tower
Of home you order the lands, and become the
    country
We all live in, its air and fallow: life
Gathers about you like the silk leaves blowing
Deep on the boles in autumn, and where it lies
The green spires prod from under like churches
    erecting
Campaniles, erecting
Ladders of bells that spring from a magical
    sowing.

Now with your chest and shoulders canted
    backward
You balance the coming that you bear before you
As a ripe pear, but not for present plucking;
A goddess, but a breeding goddess, to whom
Even the masters of the world send greeting.
Different from when, a slip of a girl, I saw you
Slight and untroubled, with a wig of wet hair,
Of plastered hair,
Fresh from the sea on the island of our first
    meeting.

                    HILARY CORKE

Matter and meaning, body and spirit, are one in the woman and in so far as she remains in touch with the Feminine in her, marriage will be seen as a way of fulfilling both her urgent body and her essential spirit. She waits to be chosen, not only by a man, but by Life itself. This waiting is not passive, but compelling; not submission but a summoning, as the negative pole of electricity compels the positive to it. She is in service but in service to the Whole, no less, and is thereby freed of narrow concern and self-enclosure.

To be penetrated is a woman's way of putting forth; to be taken is her way of giving and going beyond herself. It is not just a longing to have a man between her thighs, to fill the space within her, to have him deeply in her; not that only, but by way of the love of a man she also says *Yes* to Life itself, its joy and sorrow, both; taking life whole in this way, she is herself whole. Love for a woman is not a matter of becoming but of being who she already *is*, however darkly, however deeply; it is not so much a matter of adding another to herself but of being the One she is. It is realization, a revelation of herself.

This has been the instinctual way of most women in the past; it remains the way of many today. It does not satisfy all. This is not to be regretted, however painful it may prove both for such women and for those about them. If some women are aware of new needs that can seem more than instinctual, the ways to fulfil them will be no less natural if they are rooted in the recognition and the full acceptance of instinctual ways, even though these may no longer serve. Rejection and abuse come easily to the masculine mind; the way of woman — wherever it leads — is by way of growing out of deep roots, by outgrowing. The new needs — however they appear — are an expression of the old need for wholeness.

OPPOSITE. Charles Roff : *Pregnancy*

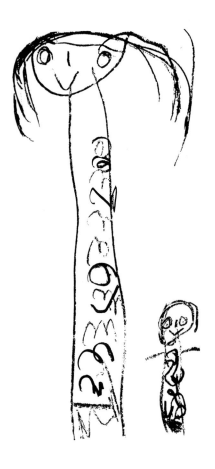

But this dependence upon the father must also be left behind. Blind obedience to another, even to what is said to be 'right' and 'good', is not a mark of maturity. A girl can know that freedom lies with limitation, in the acceptance of purposes beyond her. But the blood of the boy will suggest that Life lies in the breaking of all bounds, that freedom is to be footloose; his blood boils over:

His soul had arisen from the grave of boyhood, spurning her grave-clothes. Yes! Yes! Yes! . . . a new wild life was singing in his veins. Where was his boyhood now? . . . Or where was he? He was alone. He was unheeded, happy and near to the wild heart of life. He was alone and young and wilful and wildhearted, alone amid a waste of wild air and brackish waters . . .[10]

To take the boy beyond the safety of his parents there must be some greater calling. His mind, even as his elders, may suggest that it is wise to stay, so that what moves him to adventure forward must be otherwise, other than all he has hitherto known. For the boy it is a girl, all that he is not or seems not to be:

However many and however varied the ways that women grow and go, they will be the ways of women, not those of men. The same need for wholeness directs and determines the lives of all men, but they will go differently about it.

The infant boy has a different beginning to the girl. Born of woman he is born of a stranger. His sense of estrangement can only increase as he becomes more aware of himself as other than his mother. For that reason he may be forever haunted by the feminine. The dream of fair women may come early to him in the shape of a princess, perhaps in the clutch of an ogre, and himself as the hero who will save her. He is even then moving from his mother to another aspect of the Feminine. But he must venture beyond fairy tales and dreams. He must go alone in the way of that single sperm that raced ahead of all others to make him. He must go from his mother and for a while his father will allow identification and strengthen his resolve by example (it is to be hoped) of one who is adult and able to stand alone in the world.

A girl stood before him in midstream, alone and still, gazing out to sea. She seemed like one whom magic had changed into the likeness of a strange and beautiful seabird . . . She was alone and still, gazing out to sea; and when she felt his presence and the worship of his eyes turned to him in quiet suffrance of his gaze, without shame or wantonness. Long, long she suffered his gaze and then quietly withdrew her eyes from his and bent them towards the stream, gently stirring the water with her foot hither and thither . . . Heavenly God! cried Stephen's soul, in an outburst of profane joy. He turned away from her suddenly and set off across the strand. His cheeks were aflame; his body was aglow; his limbs were trembling. On and on and on and on he strode, far out over the sands, singing wildly to the sea, crying to greet the advent of the life that had cried to him. Her image had passed into his soul for ever and no word had broken the holy silence of his ecstasy. Her eyes had called him and his soul had leaped at the call. To live, to err, to fall, to triumph, to recreate life out of life![11]

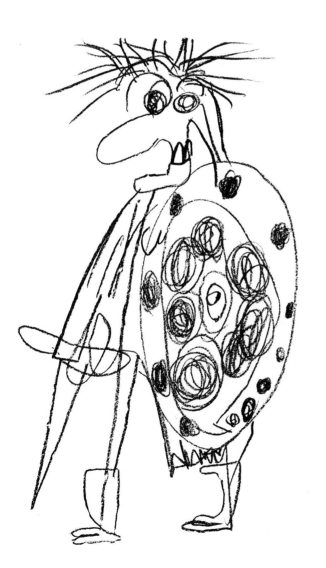

By way of error and glory, the boy will go with that bright image of a girl. As he grows into a man, so she will grow with him, within him, into a woman, strange and beautiful as ever, calling him always. He is rent by longing, made restless, seeking her in many places, in strange beds perhaps, until he can come to discover where she truly lies: within him.

It is not knowledge to be gained, but a fact to be found for himself. Though he may possess many women, the Feminine is not thereby possessed, is not the possession of any man. The Feminine *is*, and is revealed only in so far as a man finds himself, allows all that is dark and other in him. The Feminine will forever be strange for him, but need not remain a stranger.

OPPOSITE LEFT. Shana Taylor (age 3) : *Mother & child*
LEFT TO RIGHT. Noah Taylor (age 6) : *Knight to the Rescue / Simply Horrid Ogre / Princess of India*

89

That discovery of the Woman within will come to most men by way of a woman in all her error and glory. The meeting with the Feminine cannot be avoided without avoiding Life itself. One can scramble for safety to a hilltop monastery, hide in a Himalayan cave, retreat into scholarship, philosophy, mystical religion, turning inward from the world in search of some 'higher Self', seeing woman as a denial of that Self, a drag on all noble aspiration and purposes, or simply a dragon.

There is another way out, widespread today, that can seem to be a way in, into the very midst of women, of many women. There is safety in numbers. So a man can avoid the Feminine, who is always *a* woman, each and every one, by taking many women. He can pretend to be at ease with Woman by being free and easy with many women, coming carelessly but being always careful to go, sipping often and shallowly, so to avoid the full draught, dark and light, bitter and sweet, of *one* woman in all her immediacy, night and day. There are innumerable ways of escape, but that is all they can ever be, and the success of any one is the measure of a man's failure to be whole.

LEFT & ABOVE. Cyril Satorsky : Illustrations to *The Song of Songs*
OPPOSITE ABOVE. Eric Gill : *The Juice of my Pomegranate*
OPPOSITE BELOW. Eric Gill : *Adam and Eve in Heaven*, or, *The Public-House in Paradise*

A few men may be whole without living and bedding with women; a few. They are whole by having Woman already within them in most intimate marriage. Such men are recognized by their strong gentleness, their paradoxes, as by their ease with all women, with all men, as it is said Jesus was with publicans and harlots. A 'holy' man who is in any way ill at ease with women shows himself to be less than whole. There is an Indian sage who is surrounded at all times solely by male disciples; the accidental sight of a woman sends him upon a long fast, into a fever of ritual cleansing. On Mount Athos are many monks but no women are allowed there, no female of any species, not a cow or a nanny goat, a bitch or a female cat. On Mount Athos are many rats.

Loving life and not wanting to escape from it, most women and men will turn eagerly to one another as all opposites must, and in so doing put themselves under the sway of greater powers than their careful minds alone.

They may come mindful of one another; in awe of all that is strange and other; they may be shy and hesitant, bearing flowers and meaning only gentleness, only to find themselves of a sudden lifted and hurled down upon a bed, on a beach, amidst bracken, in the dark shadow of a summer tree, to make love *in more bestiarum*, as the theologians express it — 'in the manner of beasts'.

*I would lead thee, and bring thee into my
mother's house, who would instruct me; I would
cause thee to drink of spiced wine, of the juice of
my pomegranate . . .*

The Song of Songs

Theology is a 'masculine' pastime and, to the mind in all the pride and certainty of its superiority over the body, to be as the beasts of the field must seem a great indignity. 'Bestiality' is a term of abuse in the mouths of those who fear the leap and likely escape of the wild creature that is caged in them, who cannot allow the animal they are, whatever else they may also be.

For men at ease in their bodies and so with the Woman within them, as for women whose minds have not split them in two, it is no shame at all to be animal; it can even bring relief in a world where all else seems calculated and under the strict control of the human mind. Even so, a man may well lift off the woman he has lain with and come to mind again, wondering with some alarm what on earth could have so terribly transported him.

A woman may wonder also, but with less alarm. Long familiar with the body's ways, and obedient to its imperious demands, she is also without man's need of words, without his want of understanding how and what and why. It is enough for her that the Word *is* and is made flesh in her. Without seeking knowledge of the body, she has bodily knowledge. All that matters is proved upon her pulse, takes shape in her, as the aftermath of her meeting with a man may show. The man may move on at the end of an 'affair' that may prove for the woman the beginning of a whole new way of life, wholly given to the life of

another. The story of mankind over five hundred million years will be retold in the next nine months of her body as it swells with all the many forms of the past: amoeba, fish and reptile, mammal and, at the last, man, that animal with the ambiguous gift of awareness.

Although she must bear the burden alone and will do it gladly, a woman will wish to share it with the man who brought it. Marriage is the creation of women. For some men it may be little more than a sexual need that leads them at the start to accept the limitation of marriage. For a woman this can never be enough; her biological need can be served by one man as another, but marriage can seem the way to the meaning of her life, to her place in society and in the scheme of things, as woman, as wife, as mother.

For some women and men, marriage may be more than that, having a sense of fatality as inexplicable as it is certain. They are impelled by sexual needs also, but these are part of the larger demand of wholeness. A single glance may be enough for a woman and a man to see in one

another the image of that Other who will finally be found only within themselves. There is no denying such marriages, whether they are confirmed in a cathedral or made in a wild wood or a small city room without benefit of priestly blessing. They start with a glance and are not ended by all the hardships and hazards of a shared life. Thrust out of the paradise of their first meeting by greater knowledge of one another and of themselves, they accept the cross and the blessing of being in the world with one another in indissoluble marriage through all dark and daylight.

ABOVE. Rembrandt : *The Bridal Couple*
OPPOSITE. Russell Lee : *Wedding anniversary*, Italy

But marriage between a woman and a man is not in itself a certain good. Nothing is certain except each one's need to grow and flower and be whole. The happiness of a marriage may prove an impulse to that further growth, the joy it brings brimming over, spilling into other ways. But a happy marriage may also come to offer only security and shelter from loneliness, or even the semblance of wholeness in having one's apparent other half at one's side; content with this the woman and the man may be halted in their growth. What was good at the start will then no longer be so. Good is what grows.

A woman in marrying comes into her own; it can seem the fulfilment of that feminine being which calls for joining and for the furtherance of life on earth. As wife and mother, she is *being* herself, expressing that Woman within, her very soul.

For a man, however, marriage can seem more a way of *becoming* himself. Woman, it has been said, is the soul of man. And marriage can seem the end of that quest upon which he ventured when he left the safe confines of his mother. He may have lived dangerously, seeking many women along the way, and now in marriage it can seem that he has found the one woman needed. The search is not ended, however, for the woman is at his side at most; what he seeks is within.

Marriage does not come as easily to a man as to a woman, but comes of his understanding, after the trial and error of licence perhaps, that in the way of all opposites, freedom comes with limitation — an understanding that is itself the growth of feminine awareness in him.

A young girl is a deep mystery. When she enters a room something enters with her that belongs to the earth and to the sun, to the carnal and to the holy. A warm, earthly thing, a star of heaven. Pagan yet merry with God, a presence that wishes to be kind, but opens a door to sorrow.
T.F. POWYS *: Kindness in a Corner*

So at its simplest: a strong man may marry a gentle woman, and it can seem simply the attraction of opposites for one another. It is that, but it is more deeply out of the man's need to complement his strength with gentleness, so to be whole. In marrying he gains gentleness, though it is still outside him, at his side.

The strong man who at the start looks to his wife for the gentleness he lacks must therefore sometime cease to look outside himself, no longer lean upon another, but withdraw his projection in order to come upon gentleness in himself. It may happen easily by the example and presence of his gentle wife. It may as well be forced upon him by the shock of occasions of savagery in a woman whom he had thought to be only and always gentle, but who is no longer able or willing to bear the burden of her husband's projection, of his need; having needs of her own to be whole, to be more than one-sidedly submissive and gentle. A man can be surprised by the savagery of a woman, and wish to see it as a temporary derangement of her senses, as a momentary fall from that ideal woman of his imagination and need. Savagery is, however, essential to every woman's nature (as gentleness is to man's) and to the tasks she must undertake. As with the tigress and the female of all the species a woman will have need of sharp claws sometimes if she is to survive the hazards of being a woman in the world with a man on her hands and heart, a child at her breast.

OPPOSITE LEFT. Felix Hoffmann : *Young Girl*
OPPOSITE RIGHT. Edward Calvert : *The Bride*
BELOW. Charles Roff : *Head*

concubines for sensual joys, wives for children. A woman today may be all and more, and for her own sake and expression as much as any man's. Children have now become a matter of choice, and having chosen, a woman will find herself infinitely extended from the moment of giving birth and breast as an animal; in bringing up her child then she is able to express her mind, her emotions and whole human being as guide, educator, inspirer, healer, psychologist, philosopher, initiator into woods and all wild and gentle ways. Her kitchen may be alchemical; her garden edenic. And even those things that need to be done over and over can by very repetition free the woman from the need to bring thought to the tasks, allowing her wider awareness, so that hands and eyes and other senses are set free to touch and see and all else. The simple polishing of a table can prove an act of epiphany, a showing forth not only of the wood of the table but also of her own self. Men may cross their legs and close their eyes in earnest search of illumination and miss the light that is on the table, on all things, and in them. As it may be with the home of a woman, so it may be with herself, within her as within the man, a way of discovering wholeness in all ways, and perhaps most of all, at the start, in the explorations of their bed.

A woman in love may lie under her man; it is instinctive as the crouch of a lioness for whom the lion will have learned full respect; without submission the lioness will press her belly to the ground. The patriarchal mind, however, with its inability to understand the paradox of equal opposites, sees man's superior position as proof of his 'superiority'. Some who call loudly for the liberation of women see in a man lying upon a woman the stance of a conqueror above his victim, proof even of the injustice of nature in making woman who is 'simply by virtue of her anatomy prevented from being a free human being'.[12] The same patriarchal values are adopted by such women: above is *better* than below, therefore heaven is better than earth, man is *better* than woman.

To speak of the marriage of a strong man and a gentle woman is an oversimplification. There are no men who are only strong, no women who are gentle only. But marriages that are in some measure of this simple kind have enriched women as men in the past, and may do so today — the woman in being voluntarily given to the service of a loved and loving man will find herself no servant but mistress of all the many things offered by her family and her home. In a world where men are increasingly deprived of all direction and responsibility for their lives, are set to turn screws in an assembly line, are bossed by Unions, and regulated by the State in all ways, it is strange to hear from *Women's Libbers* of the restrictions of the home, for it is there that a woman can so largely determine her own hours, choose among innumerable tasks calling for endless skills and various capacities, play all the several roles asked of her, and have responsibility for her own revolt if at times she should feel reason for it.

The men of Athens knew three kinds of women: hetaerae for the pleasures of the spirit,

But a woman and a man in love and to that extent liberated will look upon their shared bed not as a battlefield but as a place for the exercise and exploration of each other and of themselves.

A woman, being feminine, may lie under, and then to allow the masculine in her, may lie above. And the man down under will find it no disgrace to be so, will feel no inferiority but only that willingness which is the experience of the feminine in him and which needs expression all as much as the masculine in him. And not only will the woman and the man in this way allow aspects of one another in themselves, but they will also extend their beings beyond human confines: the woman may bend as a beast and let the man be animal on her. They may by way of this and all other ways with one another happen upon stillness and some reach of the spirit not otherwise accessible to them.

In bed or summer meadow or in the haybarn of love there is no right, there is no wrong; there is only wild tenderness or its lack. The woman and the man in love will come to know that they are animal and much else that is ordinarily held to be 'inferior', and which needs to be included if they are to be whole. They will find at first hand the animal they are, the whore and whoremonger, sinner and saint, innocent child and ancient sage, wise one and fool. In the dark country of their double bed and in the light of their home, they may touch upon both the depth and the height of themselves. Rooted in their bodies and their earthly circumstance they grow as trees, naturally and without striving.

OPPOSITE. Berthe Morisot : *The Cradle*

BELOW LEFT. Pierre Bonnard : *The Table*
BELOW RIGHT. Augustus John : *Washing Day*

It takes patience to appreciate domestic bliss: volatile spirits prefer unhappiness.
GEORGE SANTAYANA

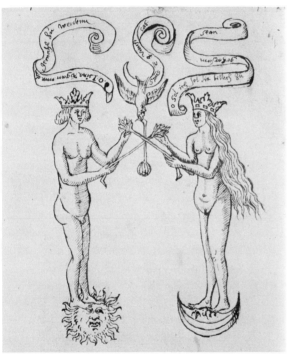

The marriage bed can therefore seem as a seed bed where all will grow if allowed. This is not to seek to sanctify the body. The body does not need to be sanctified; it is innocent always. What is needed is to bring down the lordly mind, for the mind in bed will have its part in the whole woman, the whole man, but no more. It is in the transports of the flesh that most women and men will go beyond the confines of their minds. It is because of this that a concern with sex has become obsessive in our day: in bed alone there is allowed some loss of the mind's control, some loss of self, the little madness so essential to sanity and wholeness.

The home and all it can offer, however, does not seem enough for all women today. They have accordingly gained entrance into fields that have for long been reserved for men only. In view of what men have made of the world, it must be hoped that women will increasingly have a part in its direction. It must also be hoped that they will do so as *women*. After centuries of subjection it is perhaps too early to expect much change, but there is at present little evidence of womankindly influence. Women, given the chance, act very much as men; their success being measured by their ability to do as men do. The recognition of a woman's rights has brought her, together with the right to stand up in buses and to follow a man into a room, the same vote; what is needed is that she will bring some *other* view than man's, an *other* voice.

The need to go out of the home into the world is itself an expression of some women's increasing need to be whole, to allow the suppressed or sleeping man within her. Woman is soul, so that her essential need is not to go in search of her soul but to express it, to show what she *is*. Soul is insubstantial, not an easy matter to express, so that what a woman is can only be dimly sensed by her and hardly told. It wants expression, however, in order truly to be; it is not fully realized by her until it has form and substance. The giving of form in this way is the growth of her consciousness, of the man within her. The impulse and the ability to give form and find expression is essentially masculine, and the development of this is needed in every woman who would be whole.

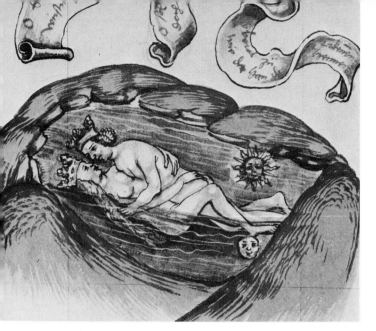

What matters, however, is that she shall give form to her own feminine being, and not ape or express the being of man.

'Understanding the masculine while abiding in the feminine, one becomes the whole world's channel,' said Laotzu. But after long ages of male domination woman can hardly know the nature of that feminine in which she must abide. The measure of a human being has been measured by man and made the measure of a man. Women have been judged by masculine standards and therefore found wanting. They have themselves accepted these standards as absolutes, and even now in calling for liberation can only conceive it in masculine terms, calling in loud and 'manly' voices for the right to be as men.

The Woman in man is his soul. The Man in woman is not her soul but only its means of expression. Man in her is her own maker, he who will give form to the Feminine she most deeply is.

A woman *is*, as a rock, a flower, as the sea itself is. But woman now needs to know *that* she is in order to be fully *what* she is, and has always been — not merely or essentially the shadow of a man, but as a woman, human and whole in herself. Men have an innate capacity for knowing, and have for long confidently known that they *are*, but what they are is not necessarily worth knowing; certainly it is not enough. Men have knowledge in abundance, but lack being; and so are in want of that Woman within who will balance and complete their necessary knowing. Understanding the feminine while abiding in the masculine is a man's way of becoming the whole world's channel.

The want of womankindliness is therefore a want both in women and in men. And if the emergence of the feminine is clearly needed to balance the over-masculinity of men and of their minds, it is no less essential in women so that they may come to know and to show to men as to the world at large what that feminine is, and all that can follow upon its revelation and relationship with what is truly masculine.

Arnaldus de Villanova : The Sun and the Moon as lovers in stages of meeting and joining to be made one and whole. 16c. Alchemical illustrations

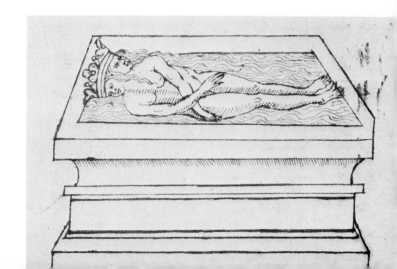

ABOVE. Ken Symonds : *Pensive nude*   OPPOSITE. Charles Roff : *Nude*

The marriage of women and men can bring a realization of the opposites they represent and contain within themselves. By way of projection, wholeness of a kind can seem to show within the wider circle of the marriage and their home. They are as two halves making a whole. But a whole is not a matter of two halves, not an addition of parts. 'The desire and the pursuit of the whole is not the desire and pursuit of another half, a complement.'[23] The whole is indivisible. It is to be found in the individual woman or man — the meaning of 'individual' is 'indivisible'.

With all her natural and instinctive needs as wife and mother satisfied, a woman may yet be haunted by the same want that a man is heir to: the need to be whole. Marriage can seem an answer to loneliness but does not in itself fulfil each woman's and each man's need to be alone, to be 'all one'.

Seemingly richly satisfied in body, in bed, in the circle of her home, her children, her work and play, there may yet come to a woman 'the image of a lost paradise suddenly set free by the music of a concertina',[14] by the glance of a stranger in a crowded room, by the sight of a gull, by anything or by nothing at all, in still moments when she does nothing and has nothing to do, when she is as nothing.

Such moments can haunt her with the sense of something numinous and other than her life may ordinarily show: 'There must be another life . . . Not in dreams, but here and now, in this room with living people . . . She hollowed her hands in her lap . . . She felt that she wanted to enclose the present moment, to make it stay; to fill it fuller and fuller with the past, the present and the future, until it shone, whole, bright, deep with understanding.'[15]

100

Such a vision of wholeness that is not to be achieved as with the ordinary dreams and desires of men, but is to be realized here and now, if one could only see it, if one could only *be* it, haunts us all, women and men.

Marriage may help to bring about that wholeness. But nothing is certain except that we come to life by participation, by meeting and staying with all that seems other and strange. We cannot grow by avoidance, so that those who are alone out of fear or from a wish not to be disturbed must suffer the lack of wholeness. Meister Eckhart told in an old language what is always true: 'Many good gifts, received in virginity, are not brought to birth in wifely fruitfulness by which God is greatly pleased. The gifts decay and come to nothing, so that the man is never blessed or bettered by them. The virgin in him is useless when it does not ripen into the wife who is fruitful.'

There are, however, other women, other men, who are not alone out of virginal avoidance, but out of the departure or death of the other, or out of the want of meeting with that other who can seem truly opposite and complementary. There are those who, for other causes than avoidance, elect to be alone. Patriarchal attitudes have given little respect to the single woman and she has suffered accordingly. But the way of inward marriage is in no way denied to her or to the single man; on the contrary, their very loneliness may make it more urgent than it can seem for those who are happily married. The way of wholeness is the way of the Feminine, and one may be whole by opening oneself to loneliness, allowing oneself to be penetrated by loneliness, all as much as by embracing another. 'This darkness I acknowledge mine,' is a marriage vow that can be uttered by a woman or a man alone, as much as by any married pair.

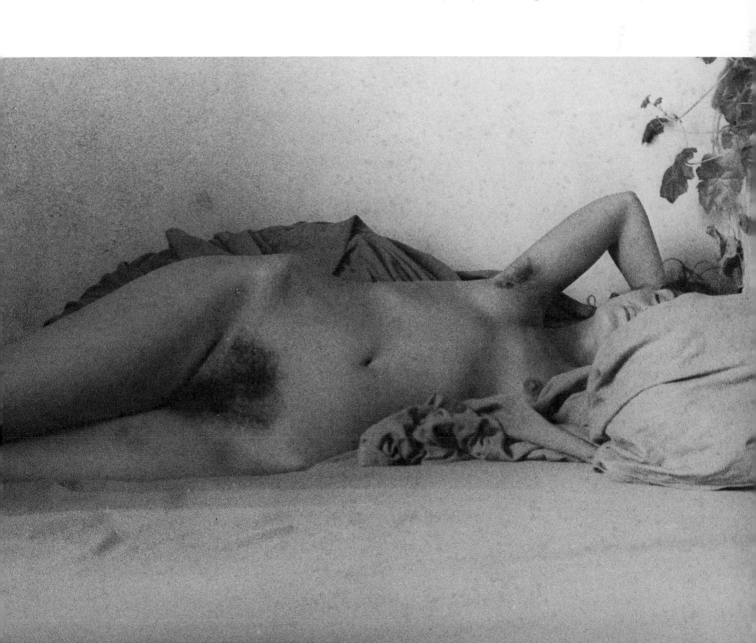

Gender is a much wider term than sex: whether human beings are male or female they have to learn the same essential lesson: that they must be feminine before they can hope with success to be masculine: they must be contemplative before they can hope to be wisely and graciously active: they must receive before they attempt to give.
GERALD VANN

But for most, the way is by ordinary everyday marriage, through all its ages and stages, its joys and vicissitudes. For some women and men it can seem they were brought together in order to learn to be alone. This is not to make of marriage a means to another end: a bud is not a means, it is a bud, and when wholly itself, it ceases to be itself, breaks into flower.

With the growing realization that even all the joys of marriage cannot answer the inexplicable need for another life, here and now, the form of a marriage may itself alter. The wide bed upon which a woman and a man once happily tumbled in love may out of that same love give way to single beds with a space between them that they both share. And that space may be increased by separate rooms, even by living apart, and all out of the growing of that same love that once brought them so compellingly together.

It is hard to tell of it, 'of that love which consists in this, that two solitudes protect and border and salute one another.'[16]

Perhaps it cannot be told. It is known, however, when any one is able to stand alone and yet in no way lonely, in no way apart, being so wholly in touch that no touch is needed, only to stand before, simply to be beside.

It cannot be told but it can seem celebrated in a story that has been danced in Bali by a Prince and a Princess who after long trials are at last able to come together. They advance slowly towards each other, face one another body to body, but do not touch; they dance together but do not touch; they look deep into each other's eyes but do not touch; they come close together but do not touch; so close they come together, so perfectly they move in the same dance, but they do not touch. Their intimacy is nearer than nakedness, deeper than receiving and penetration, closer even than the mingling of their bodies, the mixing of their blood, but they do not touch.[17]

102

But there is the dance of a Prince and a Princess, and here is the need to tell of a woman and a man, simply, in their ordinary lives, every day and every night. And to tell of it there seems only to be the one word 'love' — a word that is used for the way we reach out of a lack in ourselves, for loneliness and leaning on another; for the love of loving and of being loved; for possession, the holding and having of another; for pride in a child, for the idols we worship, for the ideals we serve, for that concern we profess for a world we ravage and spoil, even for God.

So there is need to tell also of still moments when love ends. The end of love can seem the ending of love, the end of things as we love them to be and so the beginning of things as they *are*; the beginning of women and men as they are, however they are and whatever; the beginning of children as they are, not as they ought to be; of the earth as it is, in sun and rain, in storm and calm; of the whole world as it is, all the wreck and the wonder of it, just as it is — a world without beginning or end, here and now, actual and always, myriad, momentary, timeless, entire.

OPPOSITE. Felix Hoffmann : *Man and Woman*

ABOVE. *Medieval pilgrim's badge*
BELOW Samuel Palmer : Drawing for *The Bright Cloud*

REFERENCES

1. MILLETT, Kate : *Sexual Politics* Hart-Davis, St Albans, 1971
2. LANG, Theo : *The Difference Between a Man and a Woman* Michael Joseph, London, 1971
3. SWERDLOFF, Peter (and Editors of Time-Life Books) : *Men and Women* Time-Life International, London, 1976
4. JEFFERS, Robinson : 'The Excesses of God' *Robinson Jeffers Selected Poems* Vintage Books, New York, 1965
5. JUNG, C.G. : *Psychology and Alchemy* Routledge and Kegan Paul, London, 1953
6. YEATS, W.B. : 'The Second Coming' *Selected Poetry* Pan Books, London, 1974
7. IONESCO, Eugene : 'Jack, Or, The Submission' *Plays* Volume I John Calder, London, 1958
8. FAITHFUL, T.J. : *Bisexuality* quoted in JOANNA FIELD : *A Life Of One's Own* Pelican Books, London, 1952
9. *ibid.*
10. JOYCE, James : *A Portrait of the Artist as a Young Man* Penguin Books, London, 1969
11. *ibid.*
12. MILLETT, Kate : op. cit
13. MANNING, Rosemary : *Man on a Tower* Jonathan Cape, London, 1965.
14. ELIADE, Mircea, quoted in SUZANNE LILAR : *Aspects of Love* Thames and Hudson, London, 1965
15. WOOLF, Virginia, *The Years* Hogarth Press, London, 1937
16. RILKE, Rainer Maria : *Letters to a Young Poet* W.W. Norton and Co., New York, 1954
17. Described in a letter to the author by Cyril Satorsky

ABOVE. *The World*. Card from Marseille Tarot pack

III *Woman as World*

The quest for Eden is a quest for unity. Beneath the profusion of polarities . . . lies the integrity of the pastoral mood. For the spirit of the pastoral is the spirit of comedy, of reconciliation: and the source of that spirit of unity in pastoral is neither man nor God, but physical nature.

JOHN ALCORN

There is only one necessary plan — the plan of nature. We must live according to natural laws, and by virtue of the power which comes from concentrating upon their manifestation in the individual mind . . . life must be so ordered that the individual can live a natural life, 'attending to what is within'. But once you begin to work out the implications of this principle, you do not end until you have abolished the state. For if people began to live by natural law, there would be no need for man-made laws, nor for a government to enforce such laws.

HERBERT READ

To glorify the world: *love makes no claim less than this on hearts: loved, lover — who is who? A nameless something praises here the Nameless, as birds the season they're vibrating to . . .*
RAINER MARIA RILKE

HEAVEN IS LIKE NO PLACE ON EARTH. In Heaven there is no earthquake or heartbreak, neither accident nor ageing, not the sun to harm us by day, nor the moon by night; there is no disturbance, no distress, no darkness, no death.

It is a place of angels. Even we are as angels there, with all our animality shed. There are no animals in Heaven for animals, it is said, have no souls to ascend. If there are then no horses in Heaven, no dolphins, no nightingales, there are no snakes either, no spiders, no wasps in the jam, no fleas for certain. There are lilies perhaps but no stinging nettles, no deadly nightshade, no hills in the way, no rainy days, no Mondays, no mud.

For some men there are no women in Heaven, since women bring trouble always and everywhere. Or, if there *must* be women — as they themselves seem likely now to insist — they are women of a queenly ideal kind who sit still and so do not move us overmuch; they may awaken dreams but not disturbing ones. They may even be worshipped, being of a high-minded beauty that inspires and even stirs, but not excessively, not too deeply, not below the belt, not between the thighs as on earth.

Heaven, that perfect place inhabited by perfect beings, is therefore without the need of love and all the bother it brings. There is no marrying in Heaven.

The earth, by contrast, is a wholly imperfect place. Where there is grass there are snakes in the grass, apple trees and women able and willing to do what men ask, even when they know it may bring little good to themselves. Even as a woman does, the earth offers pleasure but also pain for, given hearts to beat more quickly over the untamed beauty of the world, we are also given many things that break our hearts, even things of heart-breaking beauty — the new moon and rainbows and small staring children with heads too large for the fragile necks that support them, like great sunflowers on thin high stalks in the

OPPOSITE. Rembrandt : *Saskia as Flora*

wind. Every apparent good is threatened by what seems bad. Nothing comes lighted and alone, apart from its dark opposite. The earth can seem a lively place, but the fact that we must one day die makes clear that this life is *given* us; it is in our hands a little while at most to make of it what we can. But as it was not in our hands to have it at the start, so it is not ours to hold at the end. And so it seems with all things: we must take them as they come and go, must take them whole, as they are.

Our world is insistently whole. Paradise, having no opposites, is another world than this; it is half our world, the better half only. Here we must cope with both halves and they must seem contrariwise. We cannot rest in peace, but must live at best in paradox. In Paradise the lion lies down with the lamb; in paradox the lion leaps upon the lamb and lies down only with the lioness.

ABOVE. Edward Hicks : *The Peaceable Kingdom*

In such a world as this, without ideal women and with only ordinary men, we have need of love. We need to love one another now, warts and all, if there is not to be an end to us, as of those who wait in turn to come upon our going. It is hard to love when so little seems worthy of it. We could love with an ideal lasting love if only the objects of our affection were ideal and would last. Alas, they grow old as we do, adding wrinkles to their warts, or they do not grow old but die before we have learned to love them. It can seem hard to love lastingly where nothing lasts.

It is even harder to love God, however lasting he may be. However lawful, just, wise, all-knowing and good, it is clear that God has warts and worse since he can create and sustain a world in which — apocalyptical floods and winds and fires, bloody war and rapine apart — even one small child can be strangled at birth by her own cord and so be asked to pay the wages of sin without ever having had the joy of it.

In such a world under the influence of such a God, we have need of women for we all have warts. Women have a way of loving, of taking men whole, just as they are, as we must all hope to be taken. We cannot wish for what we deserve, cannot want strict justice. Law is among the achievements of the mind of man and plays its necessary part, but women have always looked kindly on lawbreakers, have softened to rogues and sinners of all sorts. In answer to prayer the Virgin Mary is said to have taken the place of women in their beds so that their hard cold husbands should not know that their wives had gone elsewhere for warmth and gentleness. Wanting in the masculine use of the mind, women lack a sense of strict justice, of right and wrong. As the last war showed, they are even capable of the crime of loving their enemies. Collaborators! they were rightly called by angry men — and not a few virtuous women — who shaved their heads to make them seem unwomanly, more like the men themselves, able to discriminate and to hate. The love of ordinary women is invariably illogical, often illegal, always alarming.

BELOW. Frank Capa : *Collaborators at the capture of Chartres*, 1944

Indonesian/New Zealand marriage

Japanese/Scots marriage

We have, however, need as never before of this womankindliness, of that illogical love. The able mind of man has brought such magnificence to the world and has most capably gone about solving the problems of living in an intransigent universe, a world man never made. Illogically, the solutions have only given rise to new problems. We have tackled these in turn and it has seemed only a matter of time, of the application of more logic, more mind, more science, before we arrive at final solutions to all problems, with nature brought to heel and all the wheels of the world turning smoothly to reveal a perfect society, final peace in ourselves as in all about us.

We have now even the promise of a final peace. The magnificent ways of the mind seem to lead logically and inexorably to a magnificent end — not with a whimper but with a Bomb.

To cure the inconvenience of warts by suicide is effective but drastic. We must find some other way. Whatever that way, it can only be found along the way. It cannot be an ideal end imposed by men who are themselves far from ideal. The world is cursed by those who need to change the world because they cannot abide themselves. Their disease is given a noble name; they speak in the persuasion of some one or other religious or political system to which all women and men must be brought, they insist, for their own good, however badly they may feel about it. The disease spreads for there are many who cannot abide themselves and so wish to be rid of their burden by projecting it upon others, upon all who are not as themselves, who seem opposed to them and so are the 'enemy', or who, at best, do not blindly follow, being fools.

To love one's enemies is the way of the feminine. To make of that actual earthly love a high ideal is the way of the masculine mind. A man will love all Humanity and will love to tell of it; a woman inclines to one man and makes wide her legs.

Something of that way and welcoming is, as with the woman, the precondition of anything new coming about. It is not all that needs to be done, but without admittance of that kind, nothing can come about. We do not love anyone or anything that we are intent upon changing. The only possibility of change lies in a changed relationship, in taking ourselves and others as we are. In doing so, we are already changed, for we have hitherto lived by judgement and rejection of ourselves and others. Admitting all, our minds can now determine what else needs to be done. It is only now that we can effectively do it.

To admit to all of ourselves and allow all others is to see old divisions as differences only, even to rejoice in them. It is moreover to find how truly we are all essentially one and the same. We are One in being many, and the world is seen to be whole, as we are, not by imposing uniformity but by containing all diversities.

Our past achievements and our present times push us now to a recognition of this one world we all are, and to the necessary realization of it. When we had bows and arrows, daggers, broadswords and blunderbusses there were limits to our stupidity. But not a few nations now have the means to the disposal of all, putting an end to the victor as to the vanquished. There were safe distances once between us and our enemies, wide seas between us and other members of the human race whom we were loath to acknowledge, except as objects of anthropological research perhaps. Our cities now contain them all: black, brown, red and yellow men stroll the white streets. Women of Cathay may come; out of darkest Africa and legendary Ethiopia, women may come to share a café table with us, even to share our beds, to marry and bring us coloured children, so that what once seemed far away and foreign becomes near and dear, not less strange perhaps, but a part of us.

BELOW. *English/West Indian parents and child.*
Photo : Charles Sommex

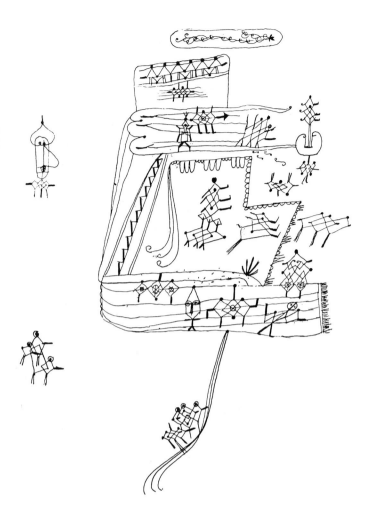

It was, however, vicariously, darkly done. Today we may know at first hand and in full awareness that everyman is a village, a whole world in himself. All that we have come to know over the centuries of the nature of man makes it impossible for anyone to separate the many elements in him, impossible to deny any of the many that make the One he is.

We will readily admit to and uphold the saint within us but hardly allow the sinner, the holy woman but not the whore. Above all, no one wishes to admit to being a fool, beneath all others. Yet it is this admittance of everyone in us that allows us to know ourselves whole and so be at ease with ourselves and others. We are made rigid by rejection; it is a strain since it is unnatural and opposed to the whole way of things, the facts of life and of ourselves.

It may seem that if we allow the sinner in us, we must surely sin, but it is not so. To condemn or deny the sinner in us makes it certain that he will sometime assert himself. All that is repressed and held down in the dark of ourselves one day rises up. Or, if the repression is strong and successful, it shows in the rigidity of oneself; one must stand as a soldier forever on guard against the escape of evil. The conqueror is not free since he must keep his heel upon the neck of the conquered. The complete and unequivocal acceptance of the murderer and the rapist in us makes it unnecessary for them to manifest themselves in murder and rape. What is already recognized does not need to assert itself.

The old walls are down, all that made us safe from one another and allowed our separate identities. The world in our time has surprisingly shrunk and we find ourselves members of one another almost as in a medieval village.

That small village was a world in itself. It had its farmer and labourer, its crafty women and men of all trades, its wise man, its scholar, its priest and publican, holy woman and whore, and somewhere in a herbal wood nearby, its curing, cursing witch. Going among them all was the village fool, laughing with those who laughed at him, sometimes abused but never denied. No one was denied. The villager, living in closest proximity to all others, admitting all others, knew the many in the one village and to a large degree lived out his many selves in the lives around him: saint and sinner were good and evil on his behalf, so that he experienced a sense of wholeness, of participation in a larger world than that of his own self only.

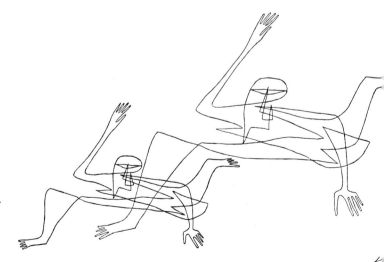

Similarly, the acceptance of the saint within us makes it unnecessary for us to be saints. The relief is as enormous as the effort was. We do not need to strain to be perfect, to try to be good, to be anything, but only be what we are. The most rare and extraordinary of all beings is an ordinary man. Women find it easier to be ordinary. When they are wholly women and are not misguided by their masculine minds, their lives are rich with ordinary things that need no special effort or attention and so may be enjoyed all the while their men are out in the world, busy about 'being somebody', achieving position and status, advancement of some kind, with all the fever of getting and the fear of losing it invariably brings.

It is sad, however necessary it may be in our times, to see women also wanting to be as extra-ordinary as men, scorning all ordinary things.

Not wanting to be anyone or anything but what we are allows us to be where we are. No longer straining our sight, not dreaming of another world, we are freed to discover this one. Wishing to be elsewhere and apart is what limits and binds us. Being ourselves and being at home we are unbounded. Knowing ourselves whole, we may then choose to express any one or other aspect of ourselves at any time. We are no longer under necessity, no longer driven by a feeling of inadequacy to assert any one aspect of ourselves or to insist on changing the world. The division between ourselves and the world breaks down. The distinction is there but it is as the difference between inside/outside, two sides of a whole. The war between ourselves and the world ends, and there is free and easy passage of ourselves into the world, of the world into ourselves.

This is not an achievement but the recognition of the way things are. All that is outside is as much us as anything inside. The interdependence of all things is the most certain and demonstrable fact; the very breath we breathe comes from outside us, and yet it is essentially us, for without it we are not at all. We do not know the full extent of our dependence on the sun and the moon, on the drift and shift of the stars, the seas and skies about us, on small foxes too, on the snakes, spiders, wasps and fleas we despise. Perhaps we can never fully know the nature and extent of the interdependence of things, for we are a part of it, *are* it all, and do not need to know how and what, only that it is so. The wholeness of ourselves is the Whole of the world, of the universe, of all that is and all that is not.

Clearly all is not well with our world any more than all is well within us, and for the same reason. It is not the lack of anything for, being whole, we are all things. But there is a lack of harmony brought about by our insistence on some things to the exclusion of others. Nothing can be excluded. We cannot spit what is distasteful into outer space and think to be rid of it; we spit into the wind and foul ourselves by so doing. Space is not elsewhere and apart, it is what allows the existence of all things everywhere, as silence allows the sounding of separate notes and their harmony. Outer space is only the other side of inner space; we are whole, being both. All that is ever altered is the relationship between things, and this alters the way they act and are. As with a woman and a man, it is out of close fond relationship that new things come about. The feminine way of welcoming and making wide is the beginning; it is not a matter of admittance as a man admits an idea and nods his head, but as a woman admits what is strange to her and allows herself to be penetrated so that things can happen in her, beyond her, by way of her, *as* her.

When we can say *Yes!* to everything, we can say *No!* to some things.

Out of the growing feminine awareness in us we will protest against the continuance of patriarchal acts and attitudes in all forms, and so for a start say *No* to all enormity, to the sheer size of things. The logical end of 'masculinity' is megalomania, 'the insanity of self-exaltation, the passion for big things'.[1] All our ills are of excess. There is a time for excess as for all things; it can seem a sickness unto life when we are young and growing up can seem a matter of self-enlargement, as persisting in folly may be a way of becoming wise.

For man- and womankind that time is no longer. For all its abuses, the patriarchal stage of the world's history was inevitable as a child's need to quit the mother by turning in obedience to the father. The need now is to be free of all parental dependence, to grow by going from home alone into the world at large; to enter it and be penetrated by it, both, and so to be whole. Wholeness knows no boundaries between woman and man, one's inward being and the outer world. There are no divisions but only differences that make for relationship, for richness and variety, all the forms and colours of things and their intermingling. In the play of the opposites is proved the interdependence of all things, little and large, infinite space and the snail on the wall.

What is done by any one is done to all in ways that are beyond our knowing, even beyond our imagining. There can be no excess of anything without a corresponding lessening, a loss of balance and harmony. The excess of the masculine centuries have been at the expense of the feminine. Awareness of this imbalance is old and deep in us; it shows in all longings for unity, in myths of a lost Paradise or prayers for a Heaven to be found one day; in the songs of mighty Solomon to a small black shepherd girl as in those of John of the Cross to his shining bridegroom Christ, and no less in the dreams of the village barmaid for a farmboy's embrace in a heaven no higher than a hayloft.

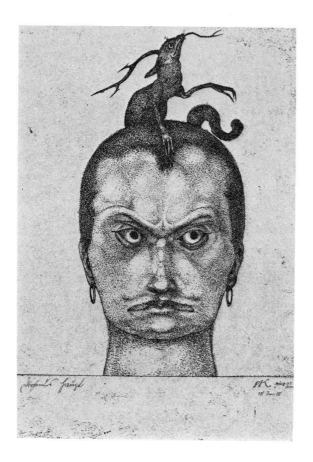

LEFT. Paul Klee : *Menacing Head*. '*Even evil must not be a triumphant or degrading enemy, but a power collaborating in the whole.*' PAUL KLEE

It may be that man's long reaching for the moon is a dream of this kind. The moon is Feminine, so that the realization of that dream can seem the outward sign of an inward need, as surely as a man's need of a woman in marriage.

That man has come at last to stand upon the moon is itself an instance of masculine excess, of that immoderate spirit of man for want of which we might have stayed back in the swamp, in the warm circle of the Mother. To reach up and out of our known selves, to dare and wish to do all that can be done is adolescent and admirable in its own way and time. It must remain adolescent, however, unless it is counter-balanced by constraint. It is a mark of adolescence to see freedom as being free of all bounds. It is a mark of maturity to understand that freedom lies with its opposite, within bounds. Form is not the denial of freedom but its expression.

It is not that adventure should in any way end. The irrepressible and even irresponsible mind and spirit of man is an essential part of the Whole, but a part only and one that therefore calls for its complement: the responsible heart and spirit of womankind. We need 'to care and not to care' both, being woman-manly and man-womanly.

ABOVE. Pablo Picasso : *Minatauromacia*

Woman has need of the carelessness of man, of his levity, lest she grow too grave and is bogged down in her body's moods, is held back by her wish to stay put. The need for security is inherent in her as one who must shield and nurture the small frail life of future generations; but in her concern for the things of the world, she may lose the ability to act upon that concern, as some who are most sensitive may so be made incapable of giving assistance; paralyzed by pity and by the sight of blood, they are unable to act to stem it.

So too, in their own way, men without womankindliness may, for all their capacities, be made incapable by lack of feeling; unmoved, they do not make a move.

The adventurous spirit of man, wedded to wider feminine concern, will naturally turn back to the earth and find there all the opportunities it could ask to risk and spend itself. The earth is in desperate need now of the mind and imagination, the invention and daring that have landed men on the barren acres of the moon.

Looking out of Apollo 8, an astronaut spoke of 'the vast loneliness of the moon . . . essentially grey . . . the bright earth . . . very very beautiful . . . an oasis in the big vastness of space . . . It makes you realize just what you have back there on earth . . .'

Without our return and the realization of our place on earth and of our part to play, whatever worth and meaning there may be in our journey away into space will be lost. The wide circling of the moon, of our going and our returning, should increase our sense of the Whole. Without that, it will seem a phallic impulse and we will claim to have 'conquered' space, using the language of those who sacked the cities and the Goddess thousands of years ago, despoiling her sacred groves and raping the women there.

ABOVE. *Give us this day our daily bread . . .*

Men without womankindliness will incline to rape. The lack of regard for the Feminine in them makes them regardless of all that is feminine in the world about them — woman herself, the earth itself. Leaving a ravaged earth behind, man then asserts his 'manliness' by moving on to rape the moon.

We have war enough on earth, enough of conquest, rape and pillage, enough now of 'manliness'. We have yet to know the earth we live on and the dark side of our own selves. We have taken ourselves to the moon but have not even brought bread to all on earth.

Even where there is bread enough, that bread is often only a semblance. Many today are without memory or knowledge of what is bread. That too has been ravaged and despoiled out of the old wish for what is only white, pure and immortal. The natural loaf of living whole wheat and water will naturally die. Man's rage for transcendence, for a purity and everlastingness unknown in nature, sends him into the laboratory for his loaf. We must stomach the consequences. The body of Jesus was likened to bread: 'Take and eat,' he is said to have said. What shall we understand of Christ the Tiger when we have only this pure, white, immortal pap in our mouths? No woman in touch with her deep feminine nature would touch it. The lack of real bread in our lives is itself an instance of the lack of the Feminine. Concern for the Feminine must bring a care for all natural and material things.

Man does not live by bread alone, but without it he does not live at all. Having bread only, however, he barely lives. It is not enough for humankind. With bread in the belly, there rises the natural hunger for that other aspect of the body that has been named 'spirit', and which is needed to make the body whole.

The minds of those who can think only in 'practical' economic and political terms are as irresponsible as they are dreary, since they do not respond to the whole human need which is for bread and roses, both.

RIGHT. *Daily Bread*, 1977

Give us this day our daily calcium propionate (spoilage retarder), sodium diacetate (mold inhibitor), monoglyceride (emulsifier), potassium bromate (maturing agent), calcium phosphate monobasic (dough conditioner), chloramine T (flour bleach), aluminium potassium sulphate (acid baking powder ingredient), sodium benzoate (preservative), butylated hydroxyanisole (anti-oxidant), mono-isopropyl citrate (sequestrant); plus synthetic vitamins A and D.
Forgive us, O Lord, for calling this stuff BREAD

J.H. Reed to Editor, *Times-Union*, Albany, NY

Given the surety of a supply of food, women and men will want to make of it more than only a means to fill their bellies; they may fast sometimes, sometimes feast with wine and candles and a rose on the table. Given simple shelter, they will want to make of it a home with impractical paintings on the walls, pots on the mantelpiece that serve no use at all. From that home they will move out into the garden to grow roses for no gain or good reason.

If talk of roses seems only romantic, let 'bread' be understood to mean all that needs to be met in reasonable measure. 'Roses' will then stand for all that cannot be simply met, cannot be measured, cannot be had by holding but, paradoxically, may come about when we no longer reach out for them but only widen our awareness and are content to contemplate.

Men have always contemplated the moon. Brutish man from the beginning, we may believe, lifted his head to the sky at night, watched and wondered over all the shifting phases of the moon, its swelling and ceasing and coming again and again. Wonder has over the ages given rise to worship, to poetry, to philosophy, to science and to simple delight. Standing on the moon itself does not, however, make it more meaningful to us than it was to those Chinamen of old who contentedly sat on moon-viewing platforms and raised their cups of rice wine to her, faraway, full and round.

Unless action has accompaniment of its opposite, contemplation, all our acts will be determined only by what they may bring us and so be made to serve only the adolescent ends of aggrandisement, gain and power. With the means in our hands now, adolescent ends can bring about the end of us.

In the race to probe space, to gain the moon and the farther planets, the super powers of the world behave as small boys boasting of the size of their 'tools' and the great distances they can piss. 'Our phallic toys have become too dangerous to be tolerated. I see little hope for a peaceful world until men are excluded from the realm of foreign policy altogether and all decisions concerning international relations are reserved for women, preferably married ones ... while men should still as in the past be permitted to control machines, it should be for women to decide what kinds of machines shall be constructed.'[2]

But that women should make wise decisions in such matters, they would, all as much as men, need to be other than they are now. War has shown how far women today are out of touch with the Feminine in them. As guardians of life, it could be expected that women would show the most spirited protest against the manufacture and sale of armaments, the proliferation of armies, of all forms of slaughter. It does not show.

If the story of evolution is true, as it seems, men have emerged out of millions of years and innumerable experiences with skills and bright minds gained by swimming in the seas, by crawling on land, swinging in treetops, standing upright on the open plain, running in the hunt, dancing round the festal fire. If one does not weep and shake one's head, one can only shake with laughter at the spectacle of man, at the end of his long evolution, standing stiffly to attention at the bark of a sergeant, marching in serried ranks, goose-stepping!

One has no choice but to weep, however, to see women ready and willing to do the same, to put on uniforms, shoulder arms and march to the same mad drum. If the other story is true and God made woman only after he had made man, it was because he wanted to do better.

Women in literature have ended wars by denying their clement bodies to men who prepared for war. In life, however, they have often offered themselves more eagerly. There is war in the world because men will it and women allow it.

Women in positions of power have yet to show themselves other than men in positions of power. A world in which rule and judgement is left either to woman *or* to men will still be a world divided and at war with itself. The need here as in all ways is not for women *or* men, but for human beings of both kinds: woman-manly and man-womanly.

Given such human beings, we can have both bread and roses, and be contemplatively active. We may then venture into space if we must, and go to the moon without guilt as we must surely go now, knowing well all that we leave behind and which is in so great a need of the attention and energies given to the 'conquest' of space. We may go to the moon then not for gain or aggrandisement but out of some over-spill of energies that have been fulfilled in the service of all earthly needs, and go gaily then as that young Russian girl who offered herself at the time of the first flight into space, saying: 'I'm all for the cosmos. I'll go too — but with a rose in my hand.'

OPPOSITE. Samuel Palmer : *The Harvest Moon*

119

LEFT. *Launching of Apollo 8, 1968*
OPPOSITE. Michael O'Cleary : *Madrona, Segovia,* 1962

Lazybones

They will continue wandering,
these things of steel among the stars,
and weary men will still go up
to brutalise the placid moon.
There, they will found their pharmacies.

In this time of the swollen grape,
the wine begins to come to life
between the sea and the mountain ranges.

In Chile now, cherries are dancing,
the dark mysterious girls are singing,
and in guitars, water is shining.

The sun is touching every door
and making wonder of the wheat.

The first wine is pink in colour,
is sweet with the sweetness of a child,
the second wine is able-bodied,
strong like the voice of a sailor,
the third wine is topaz, is
a poppy and a fire in one.

My house has both the sea and the earth,
my woman has great eyes
the colour of wild hazelnut,
when night comes down, the sea
puts on a dress of white and green,
and later the moon in the spindrift foam
dreams like a sea-green girl.

I have no wish to change my planet.

PABLO NERUDA

Meanwhile we have on earth all we need to occupy us. Man's reaching into space can have meaning if he returns then to earth and to the knowledge of where his true interest lies. The masculine impulse is outgoing. The feminine way is one of returning, earthward, homeward, inward. They are both true and lively ways in conjunction with one another, both part of the circling of the human spirit in its discovery of the Whole that is.

The controllers of Apollo 8 on its flight into space called to the astronauts: 'They tell us there is a beautiful moon out there.' The reply came back: 'Now we were just saying that there's a beautiful earth out there . . . I think I must have the feeling that the travellers in the old sailing ships used to have. Going on a very long voyage away from home and now we're headed back, and I have the feeling of being proud of the trip, but still happy to be going back home . . . And that's richer than being right here . . .'

> *We will not cease from exploration*
> *And the end of all our exploring*
> *Will be to arrive where we started*
> *And know the place for the first time.*[3]

Man, but not woman, is made in the image of God. It is plain from this that woman should be subject to their husbands, and should be as slaves.
GRATIAN, 12th c. canon lawyer

LEFT TO RIGHT ABOVE & BELOW. August Sander : *Town Official, Apprentice Teacher, Reserve Officer, Evangelical City Missionaries*
Photographed in Germany more than half a century ago, such men can seem to belong to a bygone age, but may be found among us even now, even within us.

The earth is our place; in part made, in part of our own making. We must cease to look to any Heaven or hereafter and *know* the earth as our place. Seeing it so is to protest at all men do to make it uninhabitable.

That God should tell Adam and Eve to 'be fruitful and multiply' was well said once in a wide spacious garden; it is time to protest, however, when a 'man of God' in our own day asserts: 'The family which courageously and even heroically rears a large number of people in an overpopulated area merits special praise for its virtues.'[4] Rats in crowded laboratory cages have shown such heroic virtue and gone insane. Some of the inventive powers that have taken us to the moon would be well spent in discovering how to prevent a crowding of the earth with more people than it can sustain, so to ensure also that every child will be wanted, be well fed and have space to grow and play. And to do this without laying further burdens upon woman.

The crowding of the earth is one with the problem of excessive power. The protest of the individual against the State is not only against the megalomania that the State represents, but also against the excessive control it brings. Gain in size leads to corresponding loss of control; in fear of the resultant chaos rigid order is imposed.

It is not always a matter of masculine dictatorial will but may as well be done with the best of intentions. With a motherly will, the Welfare State will plan to succour and care for all from cradle to grave; it is as a Great Breast, but being excessive and offered beyond its needful time, it can make dependent children of grown women and men. All challenge and initiative is taken from the individual, all the creative joy that comes of coping with intractable material, the little and large difficulties of daily life. For some it can even seem that the only part of their lives to which they can lay claim is their own death. All the free milk and honey of the Welfare State has not put an end to suicide.

Welfare states, being excessively 'feminine' in nature, invariably bring their extreme opposites about, taking on the alarming characteristics of 'masculine' totalitarian states. The same bureaucracy grows to administer and regulate its gifts, directives increase and the bureaucracy to direct them; laws increase with the police and courts to enforce them, and all for the declared good of the greatest number.

Bureaucracy can only govern by generalities and numbers. The individual wanders down long corridors of official offices in vain to find some one human being who can respond to his particular need; he is given forms to fill and passed on from one bureaucrat to another further down the corridor. At best he may at the end find someone who expresses full sympathy but with a shrug of the shoulders admits that he too is not responsible, is 'only doing his job', is himself a victim of The System that has no face, no mind, no heart.

123

ABOVE. Children of Dartington Hall School, Devon, c1933. *Dartington shocked the neighbourhood when it became known that the school countenanced children of both sexes bathing together in the nude. Dartington in the 1930s was an early focal point, both in debate and practice, for new attitudes towards freedom and responsibility. Society is still carrying on that debate.*
There is no bluprint, no manifesto, no tablets of law. JOHN LANE, Dartington Hall Trustee, 1976

Where authority is unavoidable, what is needed is reverence. A man who is to educate really well, and is to make the young grow and develop into their full stature, must be filled through and through with the spirit of reverence. It is reverence towards others that is lacking in those who advocate machine-made, cast-iron systems: militarism, capitalism, Fabian scientific organisation, and all the other prisons into which reformers and reactionaries try to force human spirit.

BERTRAND RUSSELL, 1919

The good of the greatest number is in no way certain to be the good of the Whole. A sense of that Whole must always bring a care for particulars, for parts, each and every one.

This is not to deny the need for order. The population of the world now demands it, as the numbers of a schoolroom must call for a kind of order that is unneeded in a home where care can be given to each child. But in this as in all areas, there is need of a balancing of opposites in relation to one another, neither being asserted or denied. The way of the opposites is the way of life everywhere, not of women and men in their homes only or only in bed, but in all they do in the world where larger numbers call for more organization. E.F. Schumacher has said:

Maybe what we really need is not *either-or* but *the-one-and-the-other-at-the-same-time* . . . All real human problems arise from the antinomy of order and freedom.

Antinomy means a contradiction between two laws; a conflict of authority; opposition between laws or principles that appear to be founded equally in reason.

Excellent! This is real life, full of antinomies and bigger than logic. Without order, planning, predictability, central control, accountancy, instructions to the underling, obedience, discipline — without these, nothing fruitful can happen, because everything disintegrates. And yet — without the magnanimity of disorder, the happy abandon, the entrepreneurship venturing into the unknown and incalculable, without the risk and the gamble, the creative imagination rushing in where bureaucratic angels fear to tread — without this, life is a mockery and a disgrace. The centre can easily look after order; it is not so easy to look after freedom and creativity.[5]

The masculine mind that directs the centre will always tend to see order as uniformity and insist that the many shall be as one. Individuals are eccentric and a threat; they have anarchic dreams, ideas of their own, unique needs, a love of

irregularities, wanting the world about them not ordered but shaped to their beings as nests are formed by the breasts of birds. Rational planners work with rulers and often with as little regard for individual needs and dreams as for hills and hollows, for the untidiness of trees. Their cities and homes are drawn on squared paper.

> *Rationalists, wearing square hats,*
> *Think in square rooms,*
> *Looking at the floor,*
> *Looking at the ceiling.*
> *They confine themselves*
> *To right-angled triangles*
> *If they tried rhomboids,*
> *Cones, waving lines, ellipses —*
> *As for example, the ellipse of the half-moon —*
> *Rationalists would wear sombreros.*[6]

The centre must insist on the reasonableness of strict rules since all that is individual is in part unreasonable and hard to rule. The centre cannot think in terms of the Whole, allowing antinomies: order and disorder, both.

And yet there are all about us examples of the marriage of opposites. All things have life and reveal it because the first impulse in each thing has found appropriate form. It is not commanded from on high, not imposed from the start. It is as a seed that grows to be a tree, rooted deep, rising high, spreading wide, taking its shape from inward impulse and from the soil about it, the water, air, sun and wind surrounding. The outcome is orderly chaos, unpredictable, inexplicable, unique.

ABOVE. Henry Moore : *Memorial Figure, Dartington Hall.* Photo : Caroline Wyndham

125

As with a tree so with man in all he truly creates. Lively form is not predetermined but arises, as the pot from the turning wheel; shaped by clay, water and all other means, including the hand, heart and mind of the potter, out of the whole of him making a new whole that never was.

The pot at the end is alive in so far as the first impulse lives through all the stages of shaping and is not overcome by excessive control. Mechanical control can make a thing of use, a plastic cup out of which one may capably drink — if drinking is seen only as a necessary and useful act, and there is not to be joy in the drinking as in the cup from which one drinks.

This is not to deny the use of things, but to warn of a world that is increasingly made of 'perfect', lifeless things that one cannot love. We may thereby lose even the ability to love and come then to look on women and men also as things that can by control be made useful for turning screws, compiling statistics, feeding to computers and cannons.

Our way with things is as our way with the earth and all upon it. 'We have to realise that every time we make an ugly lampstand we are torturing helpless metal, every time we make a nuclear bomb we are corrupting the morals of a host of innocent neutrons below the age of consent.'[7] What is feminine *feels* for things as they are in themselves, however they are; it cares for women and men as they individually, unreasonably and even ridiculously *are*. Without this folly of feeling, the rational masculine mind must see all in terms of use and accountable gain, of what all things, all beings *ought* to be, *must* be. To ensure this the mind will seek to reduce all individuals to units that can be weighed, measured, accounted and so controlled.

This will to control is as old as man's domination on the earth, as ancient as Jehovah, old as the stern lawmakers of the tribes of Israel with their tablets of stone, recent as Adolf Hitler, as immediate as the modern totalitarian state.

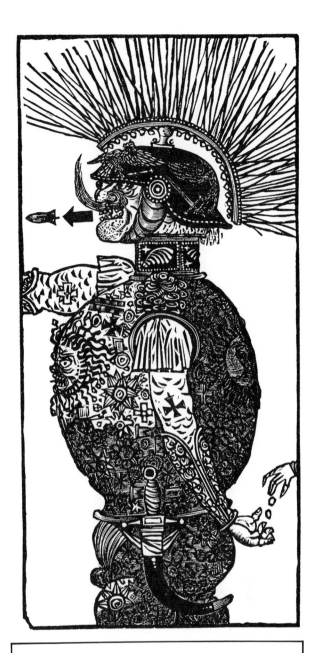

Obscene is not the picture of a naked woman who exposes her pubic hair but that of a fully clad general who exposes his medals rewarded in a war of aggression; obscene is not the ritual of the Hippies but the declaration of a high dignitary of the Church that war is necessary for peace.
HERBERT MARCUSE

OPPOSITE. Charles Roff : *Sheila-na-gig*
ABOVE. Verner Klemke : *The General*

RIGHT. *Sign of the Sixties*

The patriarchal attitude calls for blind obedience and must want the suppression of all that is unique, individual and intransigent. What is lively is suspect since life is not amenable to law, is ungraspable as running water, as the wind that blows, is unaccountable as nature herself in all her multitudinous variety. What sense can there be in swamps, in deserts, in the solitary wilderness of the world? Commonsense calls for elimination or, among the religions, for transcendence of the world.

Some men have wished for the elimination of women in their lives since women are clearly wayward, a part of wantonness. The Feminine calls for the furtherance of all the forms of life, for diversity; for some men diversity is of the Devil.

This attitude is also old. God's creation of the world and his declaration of its goodness has been explained by saying that the world as he made it was a smooth and perfect sphere, free of all irregularities, of mountains and chasms, of all warts and wrinkles. These were the effect of Adam's sin, it was said, and his sin owed to the woman Eve, that first agent of irregularity and disorder.

Men have long lamented the lack of order in the universe, have wished that the stars might be more evenly spaced and the earth be perfectly smooth, being sinless. Even in our day, Teilhard de Chardin has spoken of 'the multitude of beings' as a 'terrible affliction' and told of his faith that the world would not forever remain 'a huge and disparate thing, just about as coherent . . . as the surface of a rough sea'.[8]

The patriarchal wish for perfection and strict order has been thwarted by nature's balance of imperfection and chaos, so that what is smooth has had company always of what is rough, as light with dark, life with death. It is only of late that man has come upon the means to threaten that balance. With a blueprint in hand and a bulldozer under him, man has at last the means to fulfil the injunction of Isaiah: 'The voice of one crying in the wilderness: Prepare ye the way of the Lord; make straight in the desert a highway for our God. Every valley shall be exalted, and every mountain and hill shall be made low; and the crooked shall be made straight, and the rough places plain.'[9]

We must now cry *for* the wilderness, for the old crooked ways, for the hills and caves of Mother Earth, even for swamps where no man goes. Slowly and before it is too late, it is hoped, we learn of the interdependence of things, even of those that can seem senseless, useless, being of no apparent use to man.

Swamps, we now know, hide, harbour and support small forms of life that support larger life and so on infinitely, everywhere, always. This is our knowledge now, the findings of science. But such knowledge may also be used for further exploitation by the mind of man. It is not so much a change of attitude that is needed but the emergence of a *feeling* for things that can seem foolish to the calculating mind.

Man's capacity to feel is the Feminine in him. Its presence or its lack determines his attitude to his body and to the earth. It is lack of feeling that allows him to ravage the earth, pollute its rivers, despoil its forests.

The link of man's attitude to his body and to the world about him was shown by a traveller in the seventeenth century who, walking in a country of high hills and valleys, searched for a comparison that seemed to him sufficiently irregular and unruly, and settled upon his sexual parts:

> *A country so deformed, the traveller*
> *Would swear those parts Nature's pudenda*
> *were*[10]

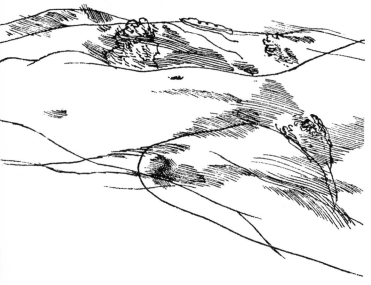

LEFT. Peter Reddick : *Landscape Figure*

Man's attitude to his body will show in his way with women and to the world about him. These are of one root, and arise out of an original 'sin' — the separation of mind and body.

In separating thought from wholeness of being, Descartes in the seventeenth century gave shape to all the centuries since, but his assertion was only a new way of expressing the older claim that man's consciousness came from on high and to him alone.

By way of that consciousness, however, we have come to know that the mind, even as the body of which it is a part, was not wholly given but has grown over the long ages, taking shape from a first impulse of which we can know nothing, and then from surrounds and from experinces of which we can somewhat guess.

It must seem that the body of man has at some time assumed forms that were kin to that of other creatures, but he is not therefore an ape that has by accident or any other means become a man. From the start and the seed of himself man has come upon appropriate form and expression. From that first impulse, out of sea and slime, out of all hazards and happenings, there have come Jesus, Rembrandt, Shakespeare, Bach.

Blind and random couplings in the deep gave way to casual animal matings on land; the female bent to the earth with the male bucking her. These made way in time for a woman and a man who stood upright looking into one another's eyes, with all the bewilderment and wonder it was to bring, all the arts of love and marriage, the outcome of children, homes and gardens, song and dance and all else. Civilization at its best has come of a woman and a man standing before one another.

Whatever else is to come of it, nothing has been wholly left behind; the past is in us, is us even now. Man's relatedness to all the forms of life is the most basic fact of his being; it is his reality, not to be sought but to be found.

LEFT. Felix Hoffmann : *Life*

Tyger! Tyger! burning bright
In the forests of the night,
What immortal hand or eye
Could frame thy fearful symmetry?

WILLIAM BLAKE

The psychological and spiritual concerns of any one individual are not to be separated from the concerns of society; and the concerns of any one society are not distinct and apart from those of all other societies, from the world as a whole. The concern of women and men for one another is part of their concern for sun and water, soil and root and leaf and tree, beast and bird, for each creature and everything in its need to give and to take from others for the furtherance and grace of all. In the consideration of human problems it is not impractical to take also to heart 'the problems of albatrosses in their shy search for the little specks of island solitude that they require in a world too full of men and rats'.[11]

'Know thyself' is an injunction that has been too narrowly interpreted as analysis, as an objective study by one or other of the sciences. Or it has been seen as the need for introspection, a means to the salvation of the individual soul. There is no soul apart from body, no body apart from the one body of the whole Universe, as

> *There is no god*
> *apart from poppies and the flying fish,*
> *men singing songs, and women brushing their hair*
> *in the sun.*[12]

Any man who would know himself wholly must come to know all that is *not* man. The forms of things in all their variety and abundance, past and present, are counterpart to the richness and complexity of humankind. With the multiplication of landscapes, of plants and creatures of all kinds, shapes, colours, sounds, smells and tastes, came the eyes to see them, the hands to touch, the ears to hear, the nose to smell, the tongue to taste, and all other ways of awareness. Women and men could not have come about by way of a world that was in any way less diverse, less rich and complex. A simple situation will only make simple demands and give rise to simple forms only. All manner of meetings, of challenges and of experiences have gone to the emergence and making of man and womankind.

They continue to make us, so that we are reduced by the loss of any form of life and landscape. The threatened loss of the tiger now will mean that man will burn less brightly; that part of his consciousness will be cut off. The loss of the wild and silent places of the earth — moor, marsh and desert, the so-called wasteland — will bring a loss of some wide, wild space in man, and the essential silence that makes him more than mechanism. And that loss of man's lively spirit is a loss suffered by the whole body of the world.

We have come to know that the loss of any one part has infinite effects upon the whole, interrupting the complex cycle of interdependent relationships. A silent spring means not only the absence of song birds but also the presence in the human body of deadly poisons. The survival of man depends then upon the singing of birds, and not his survival alone, for meaning does not lie in continuing only but in the quality of life, the wonder of things. If the cuckoo no longer comes to call that much of wonder is lost and man accordingly. And if a man does not miss the cuckoo's calling, this is proof of his loss.

ABOVE. Antonio Frasconi : *Dream tiger*
OPPOSITE. Henri Rousseau : *The Sleeping Gypsy*, 1897

130

If quality of life is our concern then wildest creatures and the most barren wilderness need no justification. It is enough that they are, and are part of the Whole. Whales and elephants are not oil and ivory; they are whales and elephants with an inalienable right to exist for no reason but that they exist.

This is not to say that all things must always be left as they are. It is often wise to do so, but it cannot always be so. Man is not simply made as other creatures; he is a maker too, and so has it in his hands to bring the natural world to ends it could not come upon without him. Out of wild grasses man has made grain and brought bread into the world; out of wild plants he has made wine and roses. The same ability allows him to destroy what is already grown and good, to disturb the fine balance of the Whole. But that there shall be destruction of some kind is inevitable if there is to be creation. It is nature's way. Life

feeds on death. Who shall say that the cut lettuce does not scream because we have not the ears to hear it? The sensitivity of plants with their own degree and kind of consciousness responding even to human thought, is now being discovered. To bring pain in the service of life is one thing; it is another matter to cause it carelessly and indifferently.

In ancient times each tree, each spring and hill had its indwelling spirit. Before a man axed a tree, he bowed before it; before he killed a buffalo, he sought by ceremony the consent of its spirit, which was the one Spirit of all. It was not a sentimental love of other creatures such as is found among us together with abbatoirs, factory-farms, battery hen-houses, hunts. It was necessary to fell the tree, but it was not indifferently done. The buffalo's death was in the service of that Life shared by all.

131

132

The earth had worship of those who bowed before the Mother Goddess in the beginning. The same regard is found today among peoples we name primitive, in whom the Feminine still survives in balance with the Masculine. We have searched and found in India a wisdom even more transcendental than our own, more abstractly male, and have overlooked, when we have not scorned, the ways of those Indians of our own west whose regard for the earth and the Great Spirit of all things might have tempered our arrogance and turned us from that suicidal path which, despite all our knowledge and skills, we wilfully take. The Navajo name for earth means 'Recumbent Woman', and the Red people sang of Mother Earth and Father Sky 'meeting, joining one another' so that 'all is beautiful. All is beautiful indeed'.

Doubtless the ancient races were in many ways blind and unknowing; it is sure that they were childlike, and we are not called to be children again. On the contrary, it is with the clearest mind aided by the searching light of science that we must now come to see that the old recognition of the one Reality in running deer and flowing rivers, in silent forests as in women and men, was based, however crudely, on the facts. The sciences that have stopped short of this finding, as the religions that have scorned the old animism, are themselves abstractions that have blinded us to the reality of things, and have allowed us to abuse the earth and all upon it.

We have ventured so far out of ourselves and off the earth; it is time to return. The way is not up and out as we have been taught for more than two thousand years, but down to earth and into ourselves, to the realm of the Feminine.

Out of the need to go beyond the confines of himself, man has looked to the faraway moon and made a woman of it, the same 'Eternal Feminine that calls us on'. But that moon is truly within. The earth is about us. The Universe is us — boulder, flower and beast; all that is to be seen, and all that is not seen to be.

Modern science gives support to early man in his awe and wonder over natural things. The mind with the many instruments of its invention has penetrated matter to find nothing material at all: 'The final substance of nature, far from being substantial, is only a complicated disguise.'[13]

Matter at the last proves to be as the Space we have sought in outer ways. We have given the name of 'God' to such immateriality, seeing it as wholly Other, elsewhere and apart from us. Immateriality may now be seen in the material things of the earth, in the guise of a swift river, a still rock, a wild rose, ourselves.

But man's knowledge wants the balance of feminine concern. It is not enough to know that all things are One; it needs to be *felt*. And not vaguely, idealistically, sentimentally, but truly felt, tasted too, smelt, heard, seen and in all ways sensed.

Before it is too late, we must come to our senses. Only our blindness could allow the desolation of the countryside by slagheaps, straight highways through curving country, the felling of forests. Only the lack of a sense of smell could allow the discharge of industrial waste into our rivers. Only a lack of taste could allow our bread and synthetic foods. Only a lack of heart could allow poverty and over-plenty, the murder of wildlife, war. Only a lack of commonsense could allow us to destroy the thin soil that layers our earth and upon which all lives depend, could allow us to foul the sea with raw sewage, oil flushings, radioactive garbage, the waste of nuclear reactors, and pollute the air about us with chemical fumes and fallout from bombs. Our children at their best are born with bright eyes and strontium 90.

Men will take responsibility only for things to which they can wholly, sensuously respond; will show concern only for what they really care. An appreciation of things as they are, warts and all, is therefore the beginning of true concern, as it is of any needed change that may come about. Patriarchal attitudes and the excessive activity that follows from them point only and always to a future, deprive us of the present which can only be experienced by contemplation, by the absence of any insistent will to have things other than they are. Contemplation takes what is given; it is present in the immediate presence of things.

RIGHT. Antonio Frasconi : *Harvest*

Playing in the world! This is what Wisdom does. And this is what they miss, those sad, resigned ones. And what they also miss — the thinkers cast in the mould of a Paul, a Marx, a Freud: the well-driven, overmasculinised betrayers of life.

ALAN McGLASHAN

destruction available to us, but absolute destruction, and the mind of man conditioned by history is unable to grasp the end of history.'[14]

The alarm has been sounded. There are protests everywhere against excessive power in all its forms, whether employed against the individual or against the earth and all upon it — all such forms being evidence of patriarchal attitudes.

But 'protests' will suggest clenched and shaken fists, slogans, banners and marches. That is often all they are. Centuries of patriarchy have so conditioned us that in protesting we assume the mask and manner of our oppressors. Revolutions start with the promise of brave new worlds and end by changing the statues in the square. Authority again asserts itself in another guise; repressive rule returns, for revolutionaries are as adolescents who still have need of fathers to oppose. Authority will end only when the need for it has been outgrown. When *Yes* has been truly said to what is new, *No* can be said to what is now old. It can even be said with love.

LEFT & BELOW : *Anti-Vietnam War demonstration*, Washington, 1972. One demonstrator pleads with others not to act aggressively. Moments later, police moved in.

Consider the lilies. Consider stinging nettles and deadly nightshade, sun, rain, rainbows and mosquitoes, humming birds and hyenas, all things bright and beastly, for they are all of us, are us. If anything needs to be done about nettles and mosquitoes, we will know what to do by way of an appreciation of their sting, by wonder at the life that is in them as in us all. Contemplation is a feminine activity and of the moment. As such it will seem timeless, and time is what troubles the masculine mind: it forever seeks more time, to gain, to achieve its ends, when it is not wondering how to pass the time, even how to 'kill' time, what to be busy about.

Without the balance of contemplation there will be nothing to be busy about, for there will be nowhere. 'We are the first men with power to destroy the planet and put an end to history. We are confronting not merely quantitative change but change in kind. There is not only more

It has been said in our times by the young. Manifestly more feminine with their long hair, their beads, bells, flowers and free embracing, the young have disturbed their elders. It is not only the envy of the ant for the grasshopper's careless gaiety, but the masculine mind's fear of the feminine, of all that is out of line and so likely to be uncontrollable. The careless ways of modern youth have put a question mark to many established patriarchal tenets. And not by way of argument but by another way of being. Allowing the Feminine in them, the young find themselves without enemies and so are hard to discipline and lead to war. They have made of love not the Sunday ideal of their elders but a way of life that is alarmingly without distinction of race, colour, creed or kind. Without ambition they are without the care of competition, and so lack the mainspring of modern society. They are gentle and lack fever, and so cannot be persuaded by poli-

tical fanaticisms. Having only the wish to be themselves, they are content to celebrate the present with all their eager senses.

The young have let slip established ends and ideals as easily as they have shed their clothes. What, it has been asked, will come of this new nakedness of the young? No one knows. One knows only what can come of older, respectable ways — cover-ups of all kinds, corruption in highest places, brutality in the name of law and order; slave camps in the cause of Freedom; not only wars but *righteous* wars, murder among Christians who proclaim a God of Love.

ABOVE. *Vietnam War scene*

135

The young have been seen as a threat for increasingly they have seen beyond the old façades and fine words to the wretchedness they conceal. Infallible popes will call for obedience to the Will of God, and the young understand by this that the *status quo* must at all costs be preserved. Presidents will speak of an end to war by way of 'Peace with Honour', and the young well understand that it is as when hunters tell of their love of animals — there will be slaughter. Truly it has been said that the despicable acts of men are not so despicable as the noble reasons they give for them.

The new world promised by the young seemed so bright and so right only a little while ago. The vision has dimmed. Seeming at first brave in disobedience to their elders and their ways, some young people have turned to self-styled messiahs who have bid them to 'turn-on, drop-out, get lost' by way of drugs; some have sought transcendence by way of sensual or spiritual ecstasy, or have given themselves obediently to eastern gurus, all to avoid the lively muddle of the many and be one with the One.

The bright morning has already passed for reasons that attend all ways of excess, out of the old insistence on one opposite without its complementary. The young have for the most part not acted but only reacted, so that their revolution can seem at most a romantic gesture. The feminity that moved them has since overwhelmed them for their gentle folly was without balance of masculine strength and a due measure of reason.

But the mark of those times is on us still, and they sometimes showed the possibility of another way; it was not a wholly new way but one that always needs to be newly expressed. Protesting against a war that was more obscene than most, a young American girl was once confronted by guards with levelled guns. In a cotton dress that did little to hide and nothing to defend the frail body beneath, the girl went barefoot and serene towards the grim-faced soldiers. Smiling, she stood before one of them and into the barrel of his gun she put a flower. Its effect showed in the bewilderment of the guardsman. Flower-power! Force can understand force, but not flowers. The same action was taken elsewhere and by young men too, and was told with laughter in tales of burly policemen with guns on both hips agonizingly telephoning their superior officers for instructions because they were being 'pelted with petunias'.

The flower was a sign of some other way that was neither blind obedience to brutal power nor militant opposition; it was not withdrawal by way of drugs or dropping out, nor by subservience to gurus in search of other-wordly bliss; it was a way of wide-eyed engagement, with all that the word implies of willing involvement, even of commitment to marriage.

This assumes that the foolish girl gave her flower in token of her love for the armed stranger. To oppose guns with flowers may only be a way of getting oneself shot. It is a poor choice of weapons. Violence and ideal non-violence are two ways of making war. To encompass evil is no ideal, and does not come by the declaration of love, nor by any commandment from on high. It is seeing the 'enemy' as a dark but in no way distant aspect of oneself, and evil as a part of wholeness. To allow what seems to be evil in oneself together with what seems to be good is to be whole and without need of ideal peace or actual war.

One may still be shot by those who are partial and at war with themselves. It may not be a great matter. Being whole, one has no insistent need of anything, certainly not of life without death.

OPPOSITE. Surrender to authority. *Disciples and their guru : 'His Divine Grace A.C. Bhaktivedanta Swami Prabhupada'*
ABOVE. Engagement with authority. Marc Ribaud : *Anti-war demonstration outside Pentagon*, 1967

Men repeat themselves in wars and bloody revolutions; women lack the necessary logic. But war is no longer possible for us; the only alternative to peace now is suicide.

Camus has asked: 'Is it possible to reject injustice without ceasing to acclaim the nature of man and the beauty of the world?' It is essential, and 'the real generosity towards the future lies in giving all to the present'.

If we cannot care for the world as it is, cannot celebrate by giving ourselves to all that is so generously given, taking mishap when it happens, admitting error and beginning again, we cannot know what the world *is*. In ignorance of this, we cannot know in what way the world needs to be bettered, nor be able to better it.

The insistent political will to change the world can only continue it in another form. Only to oppose is to maintain, as an old building survives by buttressing. Patriarchal attitudes are necessarily paranoic: an external enemy must be created to provide an escape from inner conflict, from the need to acknowledge darkness in us.

To see and to celebrate what *is* brings not only the will to make changes but the rarer willingness to be changed. Accepting oneself as one is, being nobody special, brings the readiness to be anyone, to play any part that circumstances may call for: being wise at times, at times being foolish, if we cannot at all times be wisely-foolish as we truly need to be.

To celebrate is not to stand apart and refuse to admit the 'tears of things'. It is to be in the world and be ready to sing gaily or sadly as the occasion calls for. Inexplicably, in singing however sad a song, one is no longer overwhelmed by sorrow for one is no longer only one's own sorry self; one is celebrant of a deeper mystery than one's own dread circumstance. Life is a darker matter than most of us care to admit, a lighter matter than we ordinarily allow.

OPPOSITE. Antonio Frasconi : Illustrations to Federico Garcia Lorca's *Ballad of the Spanish Civil Guard*
ABOVE. Mark Edwards : *Refugees from the Bangladesh War*, 1977

It may be for some to surmount the world and
womankind by becoming sages, beyond the
break of the heart and the bounds of the mind, but
for most of us reality can only lie in the responding heart and mind, ready to lower or lift at the
moment's notice. The readiness is all. The rest
comes as grace, or does not come. That is not our
concern.

To the mind intent upon self-assertion and
preservation, the response of the heart must seem
folly. So it is. The woman or the man who lives
willingly and wholly in this paradoxical world is
not as a still cross-legged sage but more as a
tightrope walker with his arms widespread. And
when the rope is shaken by the winds of circumstance, the way to walk on is to open one's arms
yet wider, not so much out of a concern for one's
own safety but simply in response to circumstance, as a gull adjusting its wings.

140

That opening of the arms makes one all the more vulnerable, but also brings balance. It brings, moreover, the ability not only to walk the rope but to walk it effortlessly, so to enjoy the walking and the world all about, from side to side, above and below; one learns 'to care and not to care'.

This cannot be taught. It can only be learned by living with care, carelessly. It can make no sense to the mind for it is folly, the way of the Fool.

Cleverness has brought us to the brink. If the world is to be saved now, it may well be by acts of wise folly. Not so much by the well-laid plans of grave and resolute men — though these may also be needed — but rather in the way of women who unreasonably love even such men and persist in that folly. It is not a way that is wholly unknown to us; it was told nearly twenty centuries ago by a strong gentle Fool among us, a man of inward marriage.

The masculine mind has, however, asserted itself over these same centuries at the expense of the whole body. To such a mind anyone who does not assert himself, who does not go forward to gain, conquer and command, must seem to be a fool indeed and his life must seem a comedy.

The masculine mind can understand tragedy. It strives and refuses to yield, succeeds and, in doing so, crows as the cock on his dunghill. If the mind fails, however, if it falls, it heavily sighs and groans, complains of tragic fate.

The Fool may also climb, may even crow but for the joy of it only. If he fails he does not bemoan his failure for he was never driven by the need to succeed. He does what he does for no better reason than that it is there to be done. When the Fool falls he is not surprised, and is very ready to join in the laughter of others at the collapse of himself. What surprises him is that in such a shifting world he should stand at all, should be able to walk, to climb, even sometimes to dance. That he should be at all is a matter of great wonder, cause for gratitude and celebration wherever he is and however.

ABOVE. Robert Wyss : *The Shadow of a Fool*

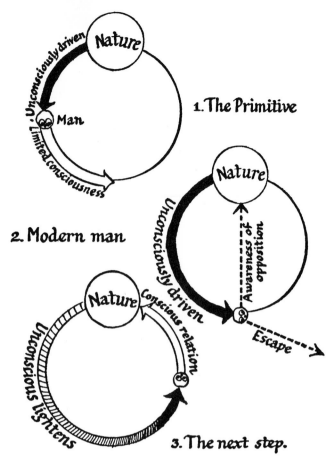

1. The Primitive

2. Modern man

3. The next step.

ABOVE. Alan Watts : *The Natural Way*. Wholeness, represented by the completion of the circle (the snake with its tail in its mouth), comes by full acceptance of the *apparent* separation of Nature and man, then by way of conscious relationship, to a realization of *actual* unity all the while.

We wonder about other worlds, even begin to wander among them. We have always looked to other worlds of one kind or another: political, ideal, supernatural. And all the while the world about us offers all possible adventure and calling; the facts and the sheer existence of things offer all possible mystery. A scientist has said that 'things are not only queerer than we suppose; they are queerer than we *can* suppose.'[15]

Life will not be found in another world if it is not known here, and will not be known anywhere as a resting place, a final answer. Having minds we will have questions, but any answer would put an end to the play of life. Life cannot then lie in any resolution of the opposites, not in any grey admixture, not in unisex or mystical Unity. The light that is on each thing can as well be known by the dark shadow it casts. When we take things as they are, black and white, in all diversity, we accept the board, the counters and the rules of the game, and can play then as life itself plays.

Once a holy man and a whole one, walking together, came to a wide river. The holy man, his head high in the air, unhesitatingly walked on across the waters to the other shore. The whole man turned and went down the bank to where the river ran shallow and so allowed all ordinary men, women and children to wade across it there. The whole man waded across with them.

To see all things under the aspect of Eternity is wonderful indeed. It is wonderful to see so much with one eye. The other eye sees Eternity under the aspect of things. With both eyes we live in a whole and fully dimensional world. We see things as they are. We may not know *what* they are, nor need to know, only *that* they are — sun and moon, earth and sky, women and men, swallows and grass, bread and cheese.

We dream extraordinary dreams, of Utopias, of Heavens and lives hereafter, of some Happy State, political or mystical. We give our lives to such dreams so that if they should end it would seem to be the death of us. So it is. It is in the ending of such dreams that waking lies and the resurrection of the body here and now on earth. We can know ourselves alive by the wonder we find in the world, in the simple acts and facts of our common day.

142

Thoreau told it in a foolish moment: 'If you stand right fronting and face to face to a fact, you will see the sun glimmer on both its surfaces, as though it were a cimiter, and feel its sweet edge dividing you through the heart and marrow, and so you will happily conclude your mortal career. Be it life or death, we crave only reality. If we are really dying, let us hear the rattle in our throats and feel cold in the extremities; if we are alive, let us go about our business.'[16]

ABOVE. *Apollo 17 view of earth from outer space*, 1972

OPPOSITE. Jose Benitez Sanchez : Huicol Indian yarn tabla : *The world as the mother who holds us all within her . . . bears us, nurtures and guides us toward death.*

143

REFERENCES

1. *Shorter Oxford English Dictionary* Oxford University Press, 1973
2. AUDEN, W.H. : *A Certain World* Faber & Faber, London, 1971
3. ELIOT, T.S. : *Complete Poems And Plays* Faber & Faber, London, 1969
4. A.F. ZIMMERMAN : *Overpopulation* quoted in JOHN PASSMORE : *Man's Responsibility for Nature* Duckworth, London, 1974
5. SCHUMACHER E.F. : *Small Is Beautiful* Abacus Books, Sphere, London, 1974
6. STEVENS, Wallace : 'Six Significant Landscapes' *Collected Poems* Faber & Faber, London, 1955
7. AUDEN, W.H. op.cit.
8. DE CHARDIN, Teilhard, quoted in JOHN PASSMORE op.cit.
9. Isiah 40.3-4
10. COTTON, Charles : *The Wonders Of The Peak* quoted by JOHN PASSMORE op.cit.
11. MCKINLEY, Daniel : 'The New Mythology of Man in Nature' *The Subversive Science* eds. SHEPARD, P. and MCKINLEY, D. Houghton Mifflin Co., Boston, 1969
12. LAWRENCE, D.H. : *The Body of God* The Ark Press, Somerset, 1970
13. ROUSSEAU, Pierre, quoted by ROBERT LINSSEN : *Living Zen* The Grove Press, New York, 1960
14. FRANKL, George : *The Failure of the Sexual Revolution* New English Library, London, 1975
15. HALDANE, J.B.S. quoted in *The Times* London, 15 May 1975
16. THOREAU, H.D. : *Walden* Collier-Macmillan, London, 1962

144

ABOVE. *The Fool.* Card from Marseille Tarot pack

Envoy: *Wo/man as Fool*

Midnight too is noon; pain too is a joy; curses too are a blessing; night too is a sun — go away or you will find: a sage too is a fool.

NIETZSCHE

Brute force crushes many plants. Yet the plants rise again. The Pyramids will not last a moment compared with the daisy. And before Buddha or Jesus spoke, the nightingale sang, and long after the words of Jesus and Buddha are gone into oblivion the nightingale still will sing. Because it is neither preaching nor teaching, nor commanding nor urging. It is just singing. And in the beginning was not the Word, but a chirrup.

D.H. LAWRENCE

I know nothing, except what everyone knows — if there when Grace dances, I should dance.

W.H. AUDEN

IF THE FOOL WOULD PERSIST IN HIS FOLLY HE WOULD BECOME WISE, said William Blake. The fool will become wise but he will not cease to be a fool; he will be a wise fool, a capital Fool.

To the solemn intentional mind it must seem that life is an absurd play. Apart from the proliferation and variety of the world, the extravagance and waste of things, there is the absurdity of other women and men in all shapes and sizes, colours and kinds, with all their wild dreams and wayward desires. Such follies apart, there is the unaccountable fact that everything and everyone comes to be only to come to an end, and even our dreams of immortality do not answer the paradox of death in life, the dark shadow that accompanies every bright thing.

But while it is clear that Life plays a game of equal and complementary forces, it can be found by joining in the game that out of the interplay of these forces comes something *Other* that, paradoxically, has no opposite, and seems to be of the nature of one only. So the life and the death of all the many things makes only for *Life*; by taking joy and sorrow, both, as they come and go, one happens upon a content that can only be called *Joy*; allowing the good and the evil in ourselves, we come upon what seems to be inexpressibly *Good*.

OPPOSITE. *Guilietta Masina as a Clown*
BELOW. *Marcel Marceau*

It makes no sense; it is not fair. In terms of the rules of the game, of the equality of the opposites, it is even foul play. But it is the way Life plays. It is so. It makes no sense to the reasoning mind; it cannot, for it is Folly.

So it also happens that a woman or a man being woman-manly or man-womanly, and by way of that being foolishly-wise, wisely-foolish, finds her/himself a Fool. She/he does not become a Fool. The Fool becomes her/him for the moment. If it seems so for more than a moment, it is because one moment of Folly has been followed by another and another. Folly is always momentary as life itself is; it is not everlasting for only death can seem that.

LEFT. *Viracocha, the Universal Father, weeping*

If there could be a God with charge over this brightly shadowed, bittersweet world we inhabit, it would be Viracocha of Argentina, whose appearances on earth are always lowly, as a ragged beggar, a fool who is reviled. He has the sun at his head and thunderbolts in either hand, but the balance of womankindliness shows in the great tears that fall from his eyes. The sun that he is insists that *life must be*! But life is painful too since it includes the death of all that lives, so that while Viracocha creates the world, he weeps for what he does. He cannot do other than what he does for he has no separate being; the world is what he is, and it is therefore compounded of smiling and weeping, light and darkness, life and death, a *whole* world. The tears that run down his cheeks are as rain to the earth and, together with the sun that he is, further the existence of all that comes and goes that Life might be.[1]

BELOW. Cecil Collins : *The Sleeping Fool*

But Viracocha, the Universal Father, is not deity enough on his own to explain such a world as ours. There must be a woman at his side, the Goddess. If he is white, she is black. And while he shines, thunders, weeps and thinks *I am*, she sits at his side, quietly as a question mark. The moon is at her feet and she has bare breasts as the Goddess of old, and her knees yawn, her thighs part to show the open wound of womanhood, not by way of plaint or sorrow, but by way of glad acceptance and to show that the way to abundant life is always into the world, involving the body and whole being.

But this is playing an old Olympian game, and God, even theologians tell us, is dead.

If we cannot find a deity to account for the way of the world, where shall we look, at the least, for someone to show us the way to live in such a world? There is Christ the Fool, 'the sign of absolute contradiction, the unbearable image of what we are and do not wish to be.'[2] But Christ the Fool has been taken from us, deprived of his Folly, lifted out of the world and set upon a throne high and apart, so that he can have little to say to us who are deep in the world and of it, who need to live in it wisely-foolishly as we must.

We shall not find the Fool amongst theologians or philosophers, gurus or wise men of any kind, but in that place where playthings may be found, in a toyshop.

BELOW. Ben Shahn, drawing

ABOVE. *Stehaufmännchen* (Little–get–up–man).
Photo : Charles Roff

The figure of the Fool may be found there in
the guise of a painted clown with his head in the
air and his feet on the ground, smiling. Shaped
like a pear, like a pregnant woman, the centre of
his gravity is set low, allowing him levity, the
ability to respond to the lightest touch. He will as
well respond to the hardest blow, spinning about,
bobbing and ducking, to return upright after and
be still again, smiling as of old.

There is no achievement in this. It is simply his
nature. 'Gravity is the root of grace.'[3]

The Fool is not strong or good in being still and
upright, nor weak in giving way. He is balanced
and so is always free to go any way, with the way
of things. In falling he does not fail; in righting
himself he does not succeed. It is simply his
nature to respond to what is, naturally; to move
when it is time to move; to be still when response
is no longer called for.

> *If the fool is 'he who gets slapped', the most
> successful fool is 'he who is none the worse for his
> slapping' . . . whenever the clown baffles the
> policeman, whenever the fool makes the sage
> look silly, whenever the acrobat defeats the
> machine, there is a sudden sense of pressure
> relieved, of a birth of new joy and freedom . . .
> the fool is a creator not of beauty but of spiritual
> freedom.*
>
> ENID WELSFORD
>
> *For what, after all, is the laughter a good clown
> brings us but the giddiness that comes of suddenly
> seeing — as if from a cosmic viewpoint — the
> absurdity of what the mighty are up to? For that
> moment, we taste the sanity of divine madness
> and become, for as long as the joke lasts, Fools of
> God.*
>
> THEODORE ROSZAK

151

> *The truth comes into this world with two faces.*
> *One is sad with suffering, and the other laughs;*
> *but it is the same face laughing or weeping.*
> BLACK ELK, *Sioux Medicine Man*

LA COMPAGNIA TEATRO DIMITRI PRESENTA:
Il clown è morto, evviva il clown!

To the mind concerned for its own standing and strong to resist any threat to itself, the way of the Fool can seem either irresponsibly careless or enviably free. The Fool smiles at the word 'freedom'; it is only a word and belongs to the world of bondage. His way is simply the way of things and his part a matter of timing. The Fool knows that he can even bid the sun to rise and have it happen, if he will himself arise at the right time to summon the sun.

The Fool is not therefore a creature only; he has part in creation, he *plays* the Fool. Life may lame him and he will *be* a lame man, wholly. Life may blind him and he will act as a blind man. So day by day he makes himself a little older, and when it is time to die, he will have a hand and a heart in it, as it were, *willing* his death. It is a game, of course. Life is that.

Tragedy and good fortune are two aspects of one whole; between them and by way of them the Fool goes over the abyss along the swaying rope that reaches from his beginning to his end, easy as an acrobat. He goes with all the seriousness of a clown about the business of earning his life in a circus of unpredictable circumstance. Life is not easy, but waking and sleeping, laughing and weeping, living and dying, the Fool lives at ease.

OPPOSITE. Georges Rouault : *The Old Clown*, 1917
ABOVE. *Dimitri the Clown*, with announcement from a theatre poster : *The Clown is dead, long live the Clown!*

153

ABOVE. Felix Hoffmann : *Pamina and Papageno : If every good man could find such little bells, his spectres would soon vanish.* From *The Magic Flute*.

An able writer once said that he wrote the first sentence and left the rest to God. A considerable artist at the height of his powers at the end of his life was able to exclaim: 'At last I do not know how to draw!' So at the end of oneself, which can happen at any moment, one can say: 'At last I do not know how to live!' even as the grey seal does not know how to swim, as the black shag dives deep without knowing how, and the gull in ignorance of how to fly, does not turn in the air to correct the curve of its wing, nor wonder whence or where or why or to what end it flies and lives and dies.

When we want nothing, we want for nothing. All things are ours. We cannot lack. When we have not joy, we have sorrow. When we have not health, we have sickness. When we no longer have life, we have death. If we deny nothing, nothing is denied us. Life never forgets us. We will forget but Life remembers us always and in all ways answers our needs. We forget to rest, but Life remembers our deepest needs and as a fond parent lays us down as small children to sleep. We forget to laugh and to weep, but Life reminds us, crowding the world with the comedy of ducks and the death of friends. And though we may forget that men will fall as surely as feathers and iron, Life reminds us when we step off a cliff and sees that we thoroughly drown. We live forgetful of death but Life reminds us in due time. Living and dying we are in the same hands. Though we may overlook it, we are at home wherever we are, as much as sages, as much as snails. It may not matter that we forget to be grateful for all things, even for nothing, for no reason, but it is in our gratitude that we are given. So it was said: 'To them that hath shall be given.'

154

BELOW *God, King and Fool*. From a medieval
manuscript

*. . . the 'Great Fool' is the forthright, simple,
uncorrupted, noble son of nature, without guile,
strong in the purity of the yearning of his heart
. . . in his own deeds light and dark were mixed.
He was not an angel or a saint, but a living,
questing man of deeds, gifted with the paired
virtues of courage and compassion, to which was
added loyalty. And it was through his
steadfastness in these — not supernatural grace —
that he won, at last, to the Grail.*
JOSEPH CAMPBELL

ABOVE Ben Shahn, drawing

A philosopher, once listing the limitations of women's minds, pointed out that: '. . . each word they speak has been formed by *man*. If woman broke away from man they would have only silence and dancing left.'[4] If men broke away from women they would have only words; their wholeness depends upon their coming upon silence and dancing. Whole women and men find a time to speak, a time to be silent, a time to dance.

With all his grandiloquent dreams turned to dust, his magnificent schemes in rubble about him, Zorba on the desolate shore began to dance. Zorba the Fool!

The mind in its place as one aspect of the whole body, brings order, clarity, liveliness, illumination, but enthroned and set apart, the mind can only blight, confuse, despoil; it can only assert itself in opposition to the body, to womankind, to the living world, the inconceivable Whole. We live within the ramparts of the mind so that when at any moment the mind ends, it is death in the time of our lives, an end to our separate selves.

There is then no one we can name or know, nothing, No-thing — the Emptiness that was before the beginning of things and is at the end of them, is now and always. And there is nothing to do now but to begin to dance: 'Men, though they must die, are not born in order to die but in order to begin.'[5]

When we cease to be our old assertive selves, we are as nothing; we are new; the Fool becomes us. The ending of ourselves is the beginning of the world for us; the chaos of creation is come again. The rest can be left to what IS when 'God' is dead — 'the morning sun, the new sweet earth and the Great Silence'.[6]

> *Solemnity sets our facial expressions and fixes our minds; we can see only what lies straight ahead of us, and but one thing at a time . . . Gaiety forces us, on the otherhand, to see two things at once, black and white, not together as gray, and yet mingled and mixed — the two interwoven, interplaying, as in the checkered fabric of Harlequin . . . I like to think that in an era of dangerous single-mindedness we may yet hold two ideas at once — that we may possess the resilience of laughter and that being serious, we may still be truly merry.*
>
> WILLIAM JAY SMITH

156

REFERENCES

1. See JOSEPH CAMPBELL : *The Hero with a Thousand Faces* Abacus Books, Sphere, London, 1975

2. EMMANUEL, Pierre : *The Universal Singular* The Grey Walls Press, London, 1950

3. *The Way of Life According to Laotzu*, translated by Witter Bynner, G.P.Putnam's Sons, New York, 1944

4. BLUHER, Hans, quoted in *Eros at Bay* by CHAR-LOTTE KÖHN-BEHRENS Putnam, London, 1962

5. ARENDT, Hannah : *The Human Condition* University of Chicago Press, Chicago, 1969

6. OHIYESA, Santee, Dakota physician and author, 1911, quoted by T.C.McLuhan : 'In the life of the Indian there was only one inevitable duty — the duty of prayer — the daily recognition of the Unseen and Eternal. His daily devotions were more necessary to him than daily food. He wakes at daybreak, puts on his moccasins and steps down to the water's edge. Here he throws hand-fuls of clear, cold water into his face, or plunges in bodily. After the bath, he stands erect before the advancing dawn, facing the sun as it dances upon the horizon, and offers his unspoken orison . . . Each soul must meet the morning sun, the new sweet earth and the Great Silence alone!' *Touch the Earth* ed. T.C. McLuhan, Abacus Books, Sphere, London, 1973

PICTURES AND CREDITS

Details and sources of illustrations are given after page numbers. Gratitude is expressed to all concerned.

FRONT COVER & ENDPAPERS (Hardcover): from Michael Adam : *The Wild Strange Place*, The Ark Press, Somerset, 1971

1: Victoria & Albert Museum, London, Crown Copyright

4: from Michael Adam: *A Matter of Death and Life*, The Ark Press, Cornwall, 1959

8: from Harold Morland : *The Singing Air*, The Ark Press, Cornwall, 1956

9: by courtesy of the artist and Henry Rothschild Associates Ltd, London

10: Richard Demarco Gallery, Edinburgh

11: The Tate Gallery, London

12L, 13R: from Michael Adam : *D.H. Lawrence & the Way of the Dandelion*, The Ark Press, Cornwall, 1975

12R: The Louvre, Paris

18L: Bibliothèque Nationale, Paris

20: by courtesy of the Trustees of the British Museum, London

21T: by courtesy of the artist and Harper & Row Publishers, Inc. New York

22T: by courtesy of the Trustees of the British Museum, London

22B: see Joseph Campbell : *The Hero with a Thousand Faces*, Princeton University Press, 1949

23BR: from *Book of the Holy Trinity*, Staatsbibliothek, Munich. See Titus Burckhardt : *Alchemy*, Stuart & Watkins, London, 1967

23T: Basle University Library, Switzerland

23BL: see Erich Neumann : *The Great Mother*, Princeton University Press, 1972

24L: by courtesy of the Trustees of the British Museum, London

24R: The Louvre, Paris

25BL, TR: see Erich Neumann : *The Great Mother*, Princeton University Press, 1972

26L:The Louvre, Paris

27: by courtesy of the Trustees of the British Museum, London

29B: The Tate Gallery, London

30, 31: see Jill Purce : *The Mystic Spiral*, Thames & Hudson, London, 1974

32: The Tate Gallery, London

34–37: from *Bilderbibel*, Zwingli Verlag, Zurich, 1961

38: by courtesy of The British Library, London

38B: see Joseph Campbell : *The Masks of God: Occidental Mythology*, Princeton University Press, 1964

39T: by courtesy of John and June Day, Dulverton

39B: from Cathedral of St Lazarus, now in Musée Rolin

40T: The Louvre, Paris

40, 41: from *The Song of Songs* translated by Harold Morland, The Ark Press, Somerset, 1972

42: at the Society of the Holy Child Jesus, London. Photo lent by Sister Hilda

43: Original size: 2.5/8×2 inches. Victoria and Albert Museum, Crown Copyright

44T: by courtesy of the Trustees of the British Museum, London

44B: The National Gallery, London

45B: Staatliches Museum, West Berlin

46: The National Gallery, London

47: Musée de Cluny, Paris

48: from G.P. Hoenn : *Betrugslexikon*, Rütten & Loening, Berlin, 1958

49B: from Peter Vansittart : *Green Knights, Black Angels*, Macmillan, London, 1969

50, 51B: see Katherine Moore : *Women*, B.T. Batsford Ltd, London, 1970

51T: Ashmolean Museum, Oxford.

52L: The Tate Gallery, London

52R: see Katherine Moore : *Women*, B.T. Batsford Ltd, London, 1970

53: Keystone Press Agency Ltd, London

54, 55T: Keystone Press Agency Ltd, London

57: Original size: 77.3/8×50.7/8 inches. The Cleveland Museum of Art (Gift of the Hanna Fund)

58: The Mansell Collection, London

62: Jaroslav Bradac, Books for Libraries, Inc.

66B, 67T: The Tate Gallery, London

68, 69: from D.H. Lawrence : *The Body of God*, The Ark Press, Somerset, 1970

70B: from D.H. Lawrence : *Look! We Have Come Through!* The Ark Press, Somerset, 1971

71T: Zentralbibliothek, Zurich

72: The Tate Gallery, London

76: The Tate Gallery, London

77: Oil on canvas, 6'8½"×9'9½". Collection, The Museum of Modern Art, New York. Gift of Nelson A. Rockefeller

78: Original: 8½"×11½". From *A Pride of Rabbis*.

79: Watercolour & pencil, c. 1900–05. 12.5/8"×9.3/4". Collection, The Museum of Modern Art, New York. Gift of Mr and Mrs Patrick Dinehart

81: Keystone Press Agency Ltd, London

82: The Victoria and Albert Museum, London, Crown Copyright

83L: by courtesy of the Trustees of the British Museum, London

88, 89: from *Alcalde*, University of Texas Alumni magazine, Austin, 1963

90: from *The Song of Songs* translated by Harold Morland, The Ark Press, Somerset, 1972

91: The Victoria and Albert Museum, London. Crown Copyright

92: Rijksmuseum, Amsterdam

94B: by courtesy of the Trustees of the British Museum, London

96: The Louvre, Paris

97: The Tate Gallery, London

98, 99: Stadtbibliothek (Vadiana), St Gallen, Switzerland

102: from D.H. Lawrence : *Look! We Have Come Through!* The Ark Press, Somerset, 1971

103B: The Tate Gallery, London

106: The National Gallery, London

108: The Brooklyn Museum, New York

109: Keystone Press Agency Ltd, London

112L: Private collection, USA

112R: Kleestiftung, Berne

113B: Solomon Guggenheim Museum, New York

113T: Private collection, Berne

114: Kleestiftung, Berne

116: from *Mutter und Kind*, Migros-Genossenschaftsbund, Zurich

118: The Tate Gallery, London

120: NASA, Houston

122, 123: from *Horizon*, American Heritage Publishing Co, New York

124: by courtesy of Dartington Hall Trust Ltd, Totnes

127: from G.P. Hoenn : *Betrugslexikon*, Rütten & Loening, Berlin, 1958

128: from Llewelyn Powys : *So Wild a Thing*, The Ark Press, Cornwall, 1973

130: from Jorge Luis Borges : *Dream Tigers*, The University of Texas Press, Austin, 1964

131: Oil on canvas, 51″×6′7″. Collection, The Museum of Modern Art, New York. Gift of Mrs Simon Guggenheim

134, 135: Keystone Press Agency Ltd, London

137: The John Hillelson Agency Ltd, London

138: from *The Texas Quarterly*, The University of Texas, Austin

140R, 141: from Michael Adam : *The Wild Strange Place*, The Ark Press, Somerset, 1971

142L: from Alan W. Watts : *The Meaning of Happiness*. Copyright 1940, 1968 by Alan W. Watts. Reprinted by permission of Harper & Row Publishers Inc. New York

142R: from a Mandala calendar. Illuminations, Inc, Massachusetts, 1978

143: NASA, Houston

146, 147: from Siegfried Melchinger : *Harlekin*, Basilius Presse, Basle, 1959

148: see Joseph Campbell : *The Hero with a Thousand Faces*, Princeton University Press, 1949

149: The Tate Gallery, London

150: from Michael Adam : *A Matter of Death and Life*, The Ark Press, Cornwall, 1959

152: Stavros Niarchos Collection

155: The British Library

156: from Michael Adam : *A Matter of Death and Life*, The Ark Press, Cornwall, 1959

ACKNOWLEDGEMENTS

The assistance given by others in the making of this book is gratefully acknowledged: to artists, photographers, authors and publishers for illustrations and quotations, and for help of other kinds, to Richard DeMarco, Charles Roff, Susan Manby, Felicity Clarke, Kim Worts, Helen Brown, the staff of the Penzance Library, Cornwall.

The poem, *Saint Augustine at Thirty-Two*, is from Clifford Dyment : *Poems 1935-1948* published by J.M. Dent & Sons Ltd, London. *A Husband's Song* first appeared in *The Texas Quarterly*, Winter 1963, and is reprinted here with permission of The University of Texas, Austin. *Lazybones* is from *Pablo Neruda : Selected Poems* edited by Nathanial Tarn (this one translated by Alistair Reid), published by Jonathan Cape Ltd, London and Dell Publishing Co. Inc., New York. Copyright © 1970 by Anthony Kerrigan, W.S. Merwin, Alastair Reid, and Nathaniel Tarn. Copyright © 1972 by Dell Publishing Co. Inc. Reprinted by permission of Delacorte Press/Seymour Lawrence.

The stanza on page 125 is from *The Collected Poems of Wallace Stevens*, published by Knopf, Inc, New York and Faber & Faber Ltd, London.

SELECTED BIBLIOGRAPHY

CAMPBELL, Joseph : *The Masks of God: Occidental Mythology* Secker & Warburg, London, 1965

The Masks of God : Creative Mythology Condor Books, Souvenir Press, London, 1974

The Hero with a Thousand Faces Condor Books, Souvenir Press, London, 1974

CURLE, Richard : *Women* Watts & Co., London, 1949

DALY, Mary : *Beyond God the Father* Beacon Press, Boston, 1974

DE BEAUVOIR, Simone : *The Second Sex* Penguin Books, London, 1976

DE CASTILLEJO, Irene Claremont : *Knowing Woman* Hodder, London, 1973

ELIADE, Mircea : *Myths, Dreams and Mysteries* Fontana Library, London, 1968

FIELD, Joanna : *A Life Of One's Own* Penguin Books, London, 1952

FROMM, Erich : *The Revolution of Hope* Harper & Row, London, 1968

FRANKL, George : *The Failure of the Sexual Revolution* New English Library, London, 1975

GOULD-DAVIS, Elizabeth : *The First Sex* Penguin Books, London, 1975

HARDING, M. Esther : *Woman's Mysteries* Rider, London, 1971

The Way Of All Women Rider, London, 1971

HAWKES, Jacquetta : *Man On Earth* The Cresset Press, London, 1954

JUNG, C.G. : *The Collected Works of C.G. Jung* Routledge & Kegan Paul, London, 1958

KAHL, Joachim : *The Misery of Christianity* Penguin Books, London, 1971

KÖHN-BEHRENS, Charlotte : *Eros at Bay* Putnam, London, 1962

LANG, Theo : *The Difference Between a Man and a Woman* Michael Joseph, London, 1971

LILAR, Suzanne : *Aspects of Love* Thames & Hudson, London, 1965

MOORE, Katharine : *Women* B.T. Batsford, London, 1970

NEUMANN, Erich : *The Great Mother* Routledge & Kegan Paul, London, 1955

The Origins and History of Consciousness Routledge & Kegan Paul, London, 1954

Art and the Creative Unconscious Routledge & Kegan Paul, London, 1959

Depth Psychology and a New Ethic Harper & Row, New York, 1973

PASSMORE, John : *Man's Responsibility for Nature* Duckworth, London, 1974

RILKE, Rainer Maria : *Letters to a Young Poet* W.W. Norton & Co. New York, 1954

SAINSBURY, Geoffrey : *The Theory of Polarity* The Adelphi, London, 1931

SHEPARD, Paul & MCKINLEY, Daniel (eds) *The Subversive Science* Houghton Mifflin Co., Boston, 1969

SINGER, June : *Androgyny* Anchor Press/Doubleday, New York, 1976

STASSINOPOULOUS, Arianna : *The Female Women* Davis-Poynter, London, 1973

STONE, Merlin : *The Paradise Papers* Virago, London, 1976

WATTS, Alan : *Nature, Man And Woman* Thames & Hudson, London 1958

Charles Roff : *Landscape with Michael Adam*